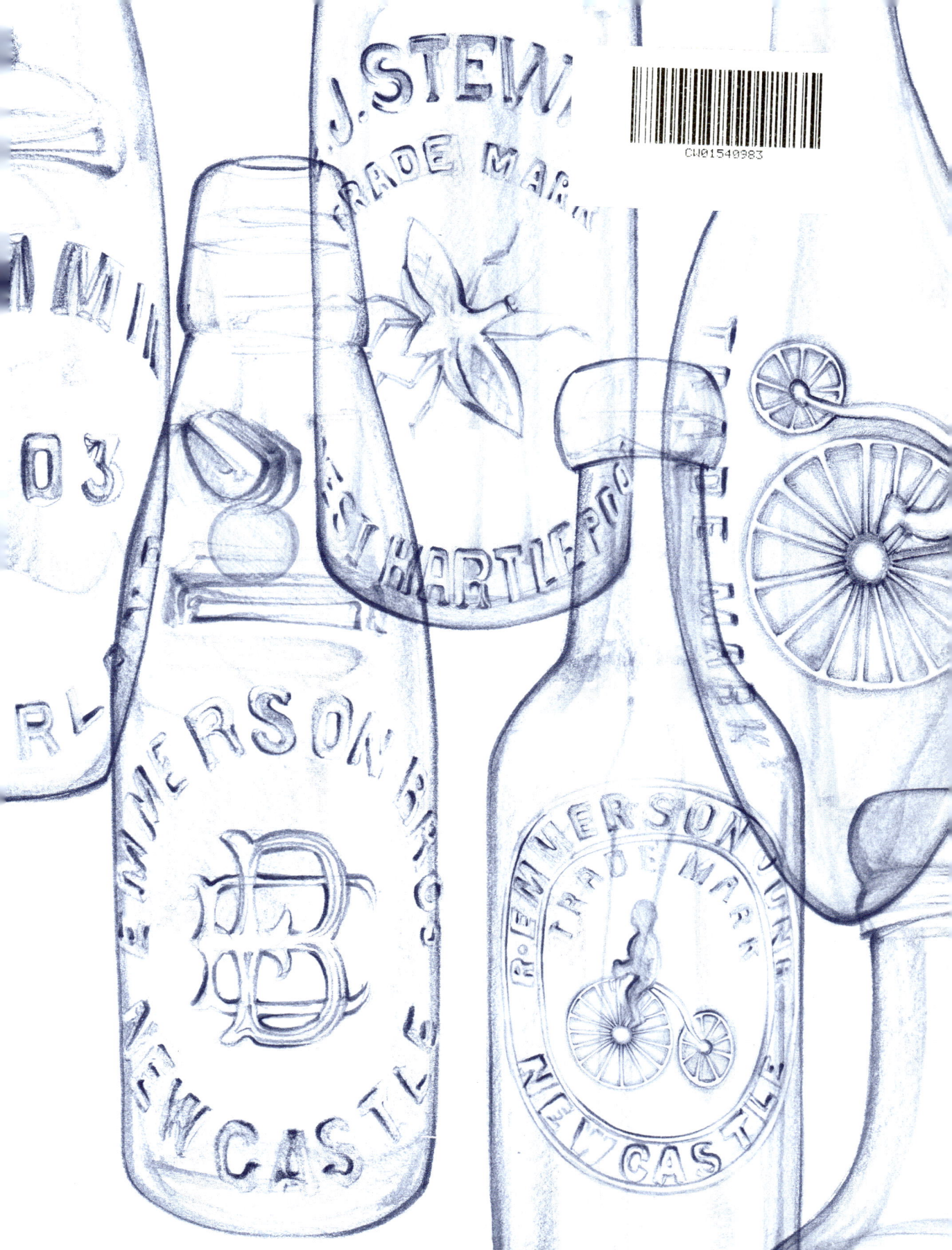

NOTHING BUT THE BLUES

Blue Glass Mineral Water Bottles from North East England

NOTHING BUT THE BLUES

Blue Glass Mineral Water Bottles from North East England

John C. Yule

Broompark Books
Durham
2016

© John C. Yule, 2016

Published by Broompark Books, 10 Front Street, Broompark, Durham DH7 7QX

The right of John C. Yule to be identified as the author of this work has been asserted by him in accordance with the Copyright, Designs and Patents Act 1988.

All rights reserved. No part of this publication may be reproduced, stored in a retrieval system, or transmitted in any form by any means electronic, mechanical, photocopying, recording or otherwise without prior permission of the author

British Library Cataloguing-in-Publication Data

A catalogue record of this book is available from the British Library

ISBN 978-0-9519401-7-4

Book layout and design by Clare Brayshaw

Prepared and printed by:

York Publishing Services Ltd
64 Hallfield Road
Layerthorpe
York YO31 7ZQ

Tel: 01904 431213

Website: www.yps-publishing.co.uk

Contents

Introduction   vii

Acknowledgements   xii

Dimensions, Capacities, Transcriptions and Illustrations   xiii

Chapter 1   The Manufacture of Blue Glass Mineral Water Bottles   1

Chapter 2   Shapes and Closures of Blue Glass Mineral Water Bottles   11

Chapter 3   Embossing, Etching and the A10 mark   16

Chapter 4   Restoration and Polishing   21

Chapter 5   The North East Firms and their Blue Glass Mineral Water Bottles   24

     John Arkle, Morpeth, Northumberland   24

     J. J. Bell, Newcastle upon Tyne   27

     Bewick Brothers, Blaydon, Co. Durham   29

     F. Bradford, Newcastle upon Tyne   31

     Bradford Brothers, Newcastle upon Tyne   34

     Crystal Aerated Water Company, Newcastle upon Tyne   37

     J. Deuchar, Newcastle upon Tyne   38

     Dowson Brothers, Gateshead, Co. Durham   40

     G. Eland, Newcastle upon Tyne   43

     Emmerson Brothers, Newcastle upon Tyne   51

     R. Emmerson Jnr, Newcastle upon Tyne   54

     Fleet, Birtley, Co. Durham   77

     Walter Forbes, Newcastle upon Tyne & Edinburgh   79

Gilpin & Company, Newcastle upon Tyne	81
Glendenning, Newcastle upon Tyne	92
J. G. Graham, Newcastle upon Tyne	94
Jas Grieves (& Sons), South Shields, Co. Durham	95
Hornsby Brothers, Gateshead, Co. Durham	97
J. Kershaw & Sons, Gateshead, Co. Durham	98
Jas McKie & Son(s), Newcastle upon Tyne	102
Newcastle & District Aerated Water Company, Newcastle upon Tyne	106
W. B. Reid & Co. Ltd, Newcastle upon Tyne	109
William Robson, Sunderland, Co. Durham	114
W. Roome, Darlington, Co. Durham	132
Ross & Co., Newcastle upon Tyne	134
William Row, Newcastle upon Tyne	135
G. T. Scott & Company, Wallsend, Northumberland	139
Shimmin, Sunderland, Co. Durham	142
Robert Stephenson, Gateshead, Co. Durham	146
E. J. Stewart, West Hartlepool, Co. Durham	147
P. Thornton (Limited), South Shields, Co. Durham	151
Bibliography	159
Appendix: Check-list of the Firms and their Blue Glass Mineral Water Bottles	162

Introduction

The title of this book may be more familiar from the popular style of Afro-American music. I have borrowed it here as it also aptly describes the subject matter of this book which is the blue glass mineral water bottles used by mineral water manufacturers in north-east England in the late nineteenth century and early twentieth century and which are now so avidly collected both locally and nationwide.

In the book I have used the term North East to define the area of north-east England which, in the period in question, consisted of the counties of Northumberland and Durham and the city of Newcastle upon Tyne. As shown on the map on page ix this area is bounded by the River Tweed in the north (the border with Scotland), the River Tees in the south (the border with the North Riding of Yorkshire), the North Sea coast in the east and the borders of Scotland and Cumberland in the west.

The hobby of bottle-collecting in the United Kingdom started in the early 1970s with the digging of Victorian and Edwardian ash-tips for the wealth of items they contained particularly old bottles. In the ensuing forty years it has grown into the well-established hobby that it is today with an active range of local clubs, bottle shows, auctions and magazines.

In the early days of the hobby with many different types of old bottles being unearthed collectors soon started to specialise and glass mineral water bottles quickly became one of the most popular and important specialties within the hobby. The range of mineral water bottles available to the collector today stretches from the Hamilton, introduced in the early nineteenth century, through to the wealth of different patented bottle shapes and closures that appeared in the latter part of that century.

Nationally mineral water bottles were made of cheap aqua-coloured soda glass and the use of coloured glass was the exception rather than the rule and the rarity and vivid colour of examples in blue glass in particular quickly made them highly prized by collectors. It is now evident that the North East as an area had a disproportionately large number of firms using blue glass mineral water bottles. Currently a total of thirty-one different North East firms are known who between them used eighty different types of blue glass bottles which is quite astonishing given the rarity and scattered nature of blue glass examples in the rest of the United Kingdom.

The map of the North East shows the locations of the mineral water manufacturers who used blue glass bottles. The largest concentration is around the River Tyne with the city of Newcastle upon Tyne having the largest number. The most westerly firm, still on the Tyne, was at Blaydon. The most northerly firm was at Morpeth in Northumberland and the most southern firms were in the south of County Durham at West Hartlepool and Darlington. The following list shows the towns and cities with the number of firms using blue glass bottles in each location in brackets.

Birtley, Co. Durham (1 firm)	Newcastle upon Tyne (17 firms)
Blaydon, Co. Durham (1 firm)	South Shields, Co. Durham (2 firms)
Darlington, Co. Durham (1 firm)	Sunderland, Co. Durham (2 firms)
Gateshead, Co. Durham (4 firms)	Wallsend, Northumberland (1 firm)
Morpeth, Northumberland (1 firm)	West Hartlepool, Co. Durham (1 firm)

Birtley was a small township in County Durham in the late nineteenth century situated on the old Great North Road some three miles north of Chester-Le-Street and five miles south of Gateshead. It was described in 1894 as "chiefly inhabited by workers from the nearby collieries and ironworks". A mineral water manufacturer from the town used a blue glass mineral water cylinder among his range of bottles.

Blaydon on Tyne lies on the south bank of the Tyne about four miles west of Gateshead and for many is probably most familiar today from the famous Blaydon Races song of 1862. In the nineteenth century it developed into a diverse industrial centre with mining, brick-making, glass bottle manufacture, engineering and chemical manufacture. Blaydon supported several mineral water firms one of which used blue glass Hamiltons and Alexander's glassworks in the town also made blue glass mineral water bottles for two of our North East firms.

Darlington is situated on the old Great North Road at the southern border of County Durham some fifteen miles south of Durham City. As the site of the world's first public railway, the Darlington & Stockton Railway, many important industries developed in the market town including a number of brewers, bottlers and mineral water manufacturers one of which used a blue glass Hamilton.

Gateshead on Tyne lies on the south bank of the river on the Great North Road opposite Newcastle to which its history has always been closely linked. It developed into a large and important town in its own right playing its part in the Tyneside heavy industries of the coal trade, chemicals, glassworks and shipbuilding. In the nineteenth century it was the site of several major breweries and mineral water manufacturers four of which used blue glass mineral water bottles.

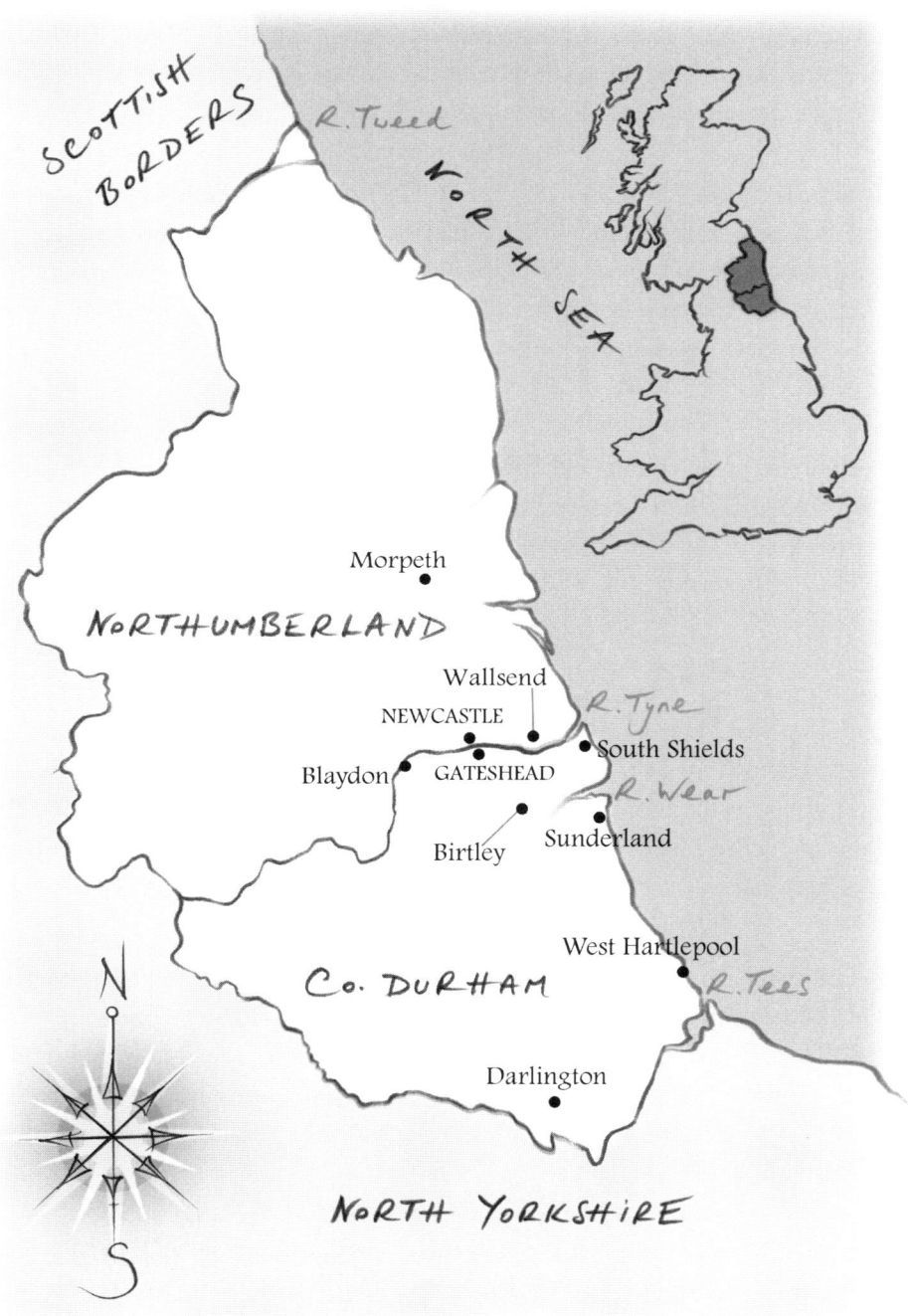

Map of the counties of Northumberland and Durham in the late nineteenth century and early twentieth century showing the locations of the users of blue glass mineral water bottles

Morpeth is an ancient market town situated on the old Great North Road in the valley of the river Wansbeck in Northumberland some fourteen miles north of Newcastle. In a rich agricultural area it supported its own brewing industry and mineral water manufacturers one of which used blue glass Hamiltons.

Newcastle upon Tyne is situated on the north bank of the river opposite Gateshead and in the late nineteenth century it was already a city and a county. Then, as now, it was the regional capital and industrial hub for the North East. It supported many major brewers, bottlers and mineral water manufacturers, seventeen of which used blue glass mineral water bottles, a significant proportion of the thirty-one North East firms that used such bottles.

South Shields lies on the south bank of the River Tyne at its mouth. In the nineteenth century it developed into an important port which eventually stretched along the river from the North Sea to Jarrow. It supported a good number of breweries, bottlers and mineral water manufacturers two of which used blue glass mineral water bottles.

Sunderland lies on the mouth of the River Wear in County Durham twelve miles southeast of Newcastle. In the nineteenth century it was a major port and industrial centre with shipbuilding, glassworks and the coal trade among its many industries. It supported several major brewers, bottlers and mineral water manufacturers, two of which used uniquely shaped blue glass bottles. The Ayres Quay Bottle Works at Sunderland was a major glass bottle producer at this time and made at least one of the area's blue glass mineral water bottles.

Wallsend is situated on the north bank of the River Tyne about four miles east of Newcastle at the eastern end of Hadrian's Wall. In the nineteenth century it expanded into a busy industrialised area with coal mining, shipbuilding and marine engineering. Its proximity to Newcastle and North Shields probably prevented it developing a bigger bottling industry but it did support a couple of mineral water mineral water manufacturers one of which used blue glass cylinders.

West Hartlepool was a nineteenth century development of the original ancient peninsula settlement of Hartlepool on the North Sea coast of County Durham. In the eighteenth and nineteenth centuries Hartlepool became an important port and the formation of the West Docks in 1845 brought with it a new development called West Hartlepool which become the major trading centre and supported a number of breweries and mineral water manufacturers one of which used blue Codds.

Why North East bottlers started to use blue glass for mineral water bottles and why that use grew to the proportions detailed above will probably never be known. Local competition between firms must have played a part and in this respect seems to mirror the enormous number of elaborately printed stoneware stout and ginger beer bottles used in the North East. However this does not fully explain the phenomenon and more will be found on this topic in chapter one on the manufacture of blue glass bottles.

At the start of the hobby in the North East the rarity of blue glass mineral water bottles, as with many other types of bottles, was not fully appreciated either locally or nationally and with the swopping, buying and selling that has always been a major part of the hobby from its earliest days many examples left the North East to enter collections in the south of England and even abroad. This is fertile ground for stories of what was found in the early days of the hobby in this country but I have only included examples in this book that I have seen personally and if this book does anything it will hopefully bring to light further examples and variations. The pace of new discoveries has slowed considerably over recent decades but with two previously unrecorded blue glass mineral water bottles appearing in 2013, both from North East firms not previously known to have used blue glass bottles, what is for certain is that we have not yet seen the definitive list of these highly attractive bottles from the North East.

Acknowledgements

The main acknowledgement must be to all those members of the Northumberland & Durham Bottle Collectors Club (NDBCC), founded in 1977, and its earlier incarnations in the North East who have unearthed examples of these bottles over the past four decades and brought them to the attention of collectors. Without their endeavours and enthusiasm this book would not have been possible.

One of the earliest collectors of blue glass mineral water bottles in the North East is NDBCC member Malcolm Sharp and an article he wrote in the club newsletter, issue 25, June 1984 titled *History of the Blues* is well worth searching out. It details his early days in the hobby in 1973 and how he paid a whole week's pocket money of 50p for his first blue glass mineral water bottle, a 10oz Bradford Brothers of Newcastle flat-bottomed blue Hamilton. He has maintained a collecting interest in blue glass ever since then and his extensive knowledge of variations is much appreciated.

Those who have made available individual items of blue glass and their knowledge of variations are James Beadle, Tony Bebbington, Ian and Nigel Best, Alan Blakeman, the late Kevin Boyle, Ralph Catchpole, Martin Embley, Phil Hall, Keith and Mark Hauxby, Ken Hemmings, Steve Kelly, Ian Liddle, Darren Lowther, Malcolm Macananey, Ken Parsons, Neil Ramsden, Stew and Jim Rickard, David Robertson, Malcolm Sharp, John Smith, Ray Spoors, Barney Stephenson, the late Howard Watson, Mark Watson, Eddie Whale.

For various items of research including census returns, family history research, bankruptcy hearings and items from local newspapers, some of which have been published in the NDBCC newsletter others received by personal communication, I am indebted to Stephen Cook, the late Terry Glendenning, Archie Miles, Mick Pickering, Mark Potten, David Robertson and Margaret Yule.

For access to research sources the Newcastle Central Library Local Studies Section, Tyne & Wear Archives, Durham City Library and Durham University Library Palace Green.

I am grateful to James Beadle for his expertise in taking the majority of the photographs of the blue glass bottles in this book. Other photographs came from Alan Blakeman (Emmerson Brothers Newcastle Codd) and from my own efforts.

The professional illustrations are from illustrator Juliet Percival of the Percival Press, Fowler's Yard, Durham City to whom I am grateful for her patience and skill.

Dimensions, Capacities, Transcriptions and Illustrations

Dimensions

Linear dimensions of bottles are generally not given as significant variations in size are found among examples consistent with bottles made largely by hand.

Capacities

The volumes I have used to differentiate the types of bottles are the standard 6oz and 10oz capacities. These are fluid ounces as defined by the *Weights and Measures Act 1824* (5 Geo. IV c.74) which standardised imperial weights and measures in the United Kingdom in response to the problems caused by the several different systems of measurement in use in the country at that time. The volumes of the Imperial System are fluid ounces, gills, quarts and gallons as below.

¼ pint (1 gill) = 5 fluid ounces (5oz)
½ pint = 10 fluid ounces (10oz)
1 pint = 20 fluid ounces (20oz)
2 pints = 1 quart
8 pints = 1 gallon

The Imperial System proved its worth and it was a hundred and fifty years before it was replaced by the metric system in the United Kingdom. However it should be noted that the mineral water trade press of the late nineteenth century shows that the mineral water trade itself often used definitions of volume inconsistent with the imperial system. For example it often used the term "gill" for a half pint capacity rather than its actual imperial quarter pint capacity and the term "split" was used variously to indicate an imperial quarter pint or capacities between imperial quarter and half pints and this usage continued into the twentieth century. This same usage was highlighted by *The Pottery Gazette* in its 1 August 1900 issue where there was a grumble that despite the Weights and Measures Act "the old usages still obtain in some districts.......in the North of England and some parts of Scotland half a pint is called a gill".

Transcriptions

All transcriptions are indented and appear as they exist in the original sources without alterations to the spelling, punctuation, underlining or the use of upper or lower case letters.

Illustrations

The illustrations of bottles in chapter five include one of each type of bottle used by each firm. The few exceptions are where illustrations would have been non-instructive and are self-explanatory. They are noted as "not illustrated".

Photographs

I have included a representative selection of photographs of the bottles covered in this book. Due to the rarity of many examples the photographs that I have included are, of necessity, selective. All the bottles shown are in private collections.

CHAPTER ONE

The Manufacture of Blue Glass Mineral Water Bottles

The majority of glass mineral water bottles of the nineteenth century and early twentieth century were made of soda glass to which the term “aqua” (aquamarine) was quickly attached by collectors from the variable greenish tinge to its colour. Even though most of the bottles we collect today were originally thrown away after use, mineral water manufacturers themselves did not consider them as throwaway items even though aqua glass was the cheapest form of glass available. The mineral water trade press which developed in the last quarter of the nineteenth century contained much discussion and argument about the importance of the return of bottles for reuse and how this could be improved. Strategies were introduced such as charging customers a deposit on bottles and insisting that any theft of bottles or breakages, such as by youngsters for the glass marbles of Codd’s bottles, must be prosecuted under the law and this was very frequently undertaken. It was clear that the cost of bottles was an important expense for the mineral water manufacturer and their loss could have a significant impact on his profits and even the viability of his business.

Sizes.	Code Word.	Usual Export Case.	Approximate Measurement for Flat Bottom Bottles.	Approximate Measurement for Egg End Bottles	Approximate Weight of Bottles.			Approximate Gross Weight.		
			Inches. Inches. Inches.	Inches. Inches. Inches.	Cwts.	Qrs.	Lbs.	Cwts.	Qrs.	Lbs.
To hold 5 ounces	*Anchovy*	2 Gross	43 × 19½ × 17½	43 × 20½ × 17½	2	0	7	2	2	14
,, 7 ,,	*Anemone*	1 Gross	36 × 18 × 14½	36 × 18 × 14½	1	1	0	1	2	7
,, 10 ,,	*Angelica*	,,	40 × 18 × 17½	43 × 18 × 17½	1	2	14	2	0	7
,, 12 ,,	*Angrec*	,,	43 × 19½ × 17½	43 × 20½ × 17½	1	3	0	2	1	7
,, 14 ,,	*Apocynum*	,,	43 × 20½ × 17½	46 × 20½ × 17½	1	3	14	2	1	21
,, 16 ,,	*Apricot*	,,	46 × 22½ × 17½	46 × 22½ × 17½	2	0	0	2	2	7

Coloured Glass One Shilling per Gross extra.

Distinctively Coloured Mouths (see page 35) Two Shillings per Gross extra.

Customer's Name, Address, and Trade Mark can be moulded on Bottles free for Orders of 30 Gross of one size; but for less than this quantity a charge is made for engraving mould.

The Packing is in all cases charged extra, except when specially stated to the contrary. The attention of Customers is called to the advantages of having these Bottles forwarded in our Partitioned Van Boxes and Cases. This System ensures the safer carriage of the Bottles, economises the cost of forwarding, facilitates the delivery of the Bottles at their destination, and the Boxes are then also ready for use on arrival.

Dan Rylands 1891 catalogue offered the option of coloured glass bottles

Although aqua glass was the standard material of which mineral water bottles were made bottle-makers did offer bottles made of coloured glass as a means of making the bottler's products more attractive to his customers. The main colours offered were green, amber and blue and the extra cost for coloured glass can be seen in the details shown overleaf from the 1891 catalogue of the well-known Yorkshire glass bottle-maker Dan Rylands of Barnsley. On today's evidence from dug examples amber and green, in various shades, were the most popular colours in coloured glass mineral water bottles with blue being very rare.

The bottles we are discussing here can be classed as hand-made in that they lacked the uniform perfection of size, shape and capacity that was achieved by the fully mechanised machinery that was developed in the late nineteenth century and gradually introduced by bottle-makers thereafter. The actual quality of the bottles in both aqua and coloured glass was thus far from good in a technical sense and paradoxically it those very imperfections in the glass that collectors today find so appealing and which can affect the desirability of one example against another. Of course from the viewpoint of the bottlers of the time these imperfections were far from desirable and the following article from the *Mineral Water Trade Review & Guardian* 18 December 1883 is one of many in the trade press of the time highlighting the lack of quality of the glass bottles supplied to the trade. It is of interest as it describes how the various imperfections came into being including noting that "the exact colour is of little consequence as long as the glass is bright and clear", a statement that will bring a smile to the face of collectors today.

BOTTLE GLASS

The quality of glass used in making bottles for aerated and other beverages says the *Earthenware and Glass Trades Chronicle*, is of much greater importance than might be supposed. Most bottlers are more particular about the colour of their bottles than they are about the quality of the glass, and yet the exact colour is of little consequence provided that the glass is bright and clear. What is required is a solid glass free from "oats" or bubbles. A "seedy" or spongy glass is to be avoided, for it is invariably weak; each "oat" is a bubble which materially diminishes the strength of the glass.

"Winds" on the surface of the glass are also an indication of weakness and should be avoided. These "winds" are generally evidence that "cullet" or old glass has been remelted with a portion of new glass and has not been thoroughly assimilated. Glass made in pots is more apt to contain "winds than that made in tanks from the fact that less "cullet" is used in making the latter.

Pot glass is made as follows: The batch is placed in the pot and melted through the night, being fed as often as required with a batch by the shearer. When melted the glass will sometimes froth considerably, when it requires some time to settle. Sometimes, in the eagerness to commence blowing, the glass is not allowed sufficient time to subside, and the result is "seedy" glass. At other times a large amount of salt water will appear over the glass, considerably retarding the melt. It such cases it is usual to fill the pots with broken glass until the salt water has all run over, leaving only glass in the pots. If the original batch had much "cullett" in it already, the addition of more generally causes the "winds" above referred to.

The other method of making glass is to melt the batch in a furnace, feeding it at intervals. The melted glass is carried off in a trough to a tank, and is taken from this tank to be blown. The glass in the tank is fined, and at all times ready to work. It need not, therefore be "windy". Of these two processes the latter produces the better quality and, provided the annealing is equally good in both cases it is safe to say that a bottle made with tank glass will prove more satisfactory than one composed of pot glass.

The hammered look that some bottles present is not a sign of weakness and is of no consequence except as far as the appearance of the bottle is concerned. The cause of this "hammered" appearance is that the glass was put into a mould which had not been made sufficiently hot and the steam from the surface has imprinted itself on the bottle.

The workmen are not all skilful in a glass factory. It often happens that apprentices are allowed to blow bottles when an order has been taken at too low a figure to allow it to be filled profitably by skilled workmen. It is misplaced economy to buy a low-priced bottle of inferior quality, for the loss by breakage will be so great as to more than counterbalance any difference in first cost.

The Size of Bottles

The traditional 6oz and 10oz volumes used in this book are the imperial quantities discussed in the prelims under Dimensions, Capacities, Transcription and Illustrations. The volume of examples of blue glass mineral water bottles has been measured, where possible, using the "brimful" capacity in fluid ounces (oz) as the standard. An amount has to be deducted from this for what the trade called "corkage" which is the volume taken up by the cork-stopper which could be quite significant. A trade press article in 1875, for example, recommended that corks should be no less than 1¼ inches (31mm) long so the allowance for corkage could be up to 1oz.

Measurement has shown that what we call the 6oz bottles generally do hold that amount brimful which, allowing for corkage, makes their actual capacity nearer to 5oz which is an imperial quarter pint. What we call the 10oz bottles have consistently been measured as holding 11oz to the brim which, allowing for corkage, would make their capacity nearer to 10oz which is an imperial half pint. Minor differences in the above figures do exist but are to be expected in handmade items along with the manufacturing issues outlined in the 1883 trade press article above. Significant exceptions to the above findings have been noted in chapter five which deals with the bottles themselves and the firms that used them.

It will be seen from the above that technically our traditional 6oz and 10oz sizes are actually 5oz and 10oz (quarter pint and half pint) and that we should probably be using these latter figures rather than the former however I have stayed with the traditional 6oz and 10oz terms.

The Colour of Bottle Glass

The glass-bottle makers E. Breffit & Co. Ltd made the celebrated blue Codds of E. J. Stewart of West Hartlepool and in 1896 an article on their glassworks noted that:

> ...in general terms the constituent elements of glass comprise silica, soda and lime mixed together in due proportions....when the batch is introduced to the furnace there is usually added to it a proportion of broken pieces of and chips of bottle-glass known as cullet and also any colouring matter – green, chrome, manganese, **oxide of cobalt** and the like – that may be required (*The Mineral Water Trade Recorder* November 1896)

The oxide of cobalt produced the blue colour and Chris Ward, a founder member of the NDBCC, noted that cobalt oxide had "such a great effect on colouring glass that only one part in 100,000 will produce a faint blue colour while one part in 1,000 produces a deep blue colour" (NDBCC newsletter issue 4 March 1978).

The Use of Blue Glass Mineral Water Bottles

We have already noted the rarity of mineral water bottles made of blue glass. This may well have been because blue glass was a colour more usually associated with poison bottles at the time as one of the many means of identifying bottles with dangerous contents. Its use, therefore, for mineral water bottles is somewhat surprising to say the least. An important article in the mineral water trade press in 1877 is quoted in Peter Douglas' *Extracts from the Mineral Water Trade Review & Guardian* Volume 1 which suggests that the vogue for the use of blue glass for bottles originated in America:

BLUE GLASS BOTTLES

The craze which prevails in favour of blue glass at the present moment in the United States is leading to some rather odd results. It should be premised that our transatlantic brethren have become impressed with the idea that blue glass possesses not only a wonderful curative influence on the physical system, but also that the quality of all liquids kept in glass bottles of the required azure tint becomes perceptibly improved. Whether there are any grounds for such a belief it is difficult to say, but some of the American mineral water manufacturers have lost no time in turning the national mania to account by advertising that they use bottles of the popular colour, and, judging from the increasing frequency of such announcements, it would seem as if the new trade expedient were found profitable. Whether the rage for blue glass will extend itself to this side of the Atlantic remains to be seen, but we confess to entertaining grave doubts respecting the accuracy of all that has been said in favour of the new fashion. If the quality of the liquid is influenced by the colour of the vessels in which they are confined, we should, for scientific reasons, prefer yellow to blue. Those who argue in favour of keeping mineral waters confined in bottles of a specified colour, with the view of neutralising certain alleged effects of light, appear to overlook the fact that such beverages are affected more by exposure to atmospheric air than by being submitted to the action of atmospheric light. But in one of the American scientific papers we are told that both English and French mineral water manufacturers have unconsciously recognised the action of light upon the quality of aerated beverages by their use of blue and green glass bottles. Of course the absurdity of this will be perceived by every practical man. The simple reason why white glass is not used is because it is dearer than bottle glass, the question of colour having nothing to do with it. Blue glass bottles are used by a few English manufacturers; but their dull and unattractive appearance has prevented their extensive use. They are more suggestive of the druggist's shop than of a refreshment establishment. It is possible that our American cousins have managed to overcome this drawback, but we hardly think such to be the case. So far as our bottling system is concerned there is little or no room for improvement, save in the actual shape of the bottles, and in this direction a considerable advance has been perceptible of late. It would be a great absurdity were the English people to be led into entertaining an idea that no aerated beverages could be of good quality unless kept in blue bottles. If such a belief were to gain ground it would involve considerable private loss, so far as manufacturers are concerned, without leading to the slightest public good. Consequently the trade should be on its guard, and should the mania make its appearance in this country, be ready to combat it with the utmost vigour, unless, indeed, more substantial reasons than those already given in its favour can be adduced.

This somewhat dogmatic article is fairly typical of the period. The manufacture of coloured glass bottles actually aided the glass bottle manufacturer via the extra tariff it brought in and from the collector's point of view today it is hard to accept the quote that blue glass bottles are "dull and unattractive" in appearance compared to their counterparts in aqua glass! No doubt the blue glass versions were sold at a higher price to the public and at this distance in time we can only presume that they proved popular in the North East. Certainly a number of the examples of blue glass bottles in this book are also known in aqua glass and surprisingly some of these aqua glass examples are rare. The use of attractive coloured glass in general by mineral water manufacturers seems much more likely to have been a marketing ploy rather than a belief that the glass colour affected the quality of the contents as suggested at the beginning of the 1883 article titled Bottle Glass at the beginning of this chapter.

The Manufacturers of Blue Glass Bottles

Many of the aqua, green, amber and black glass bottles seen in the North East have makers' marks from local glass bottle-works or from the major glassworks of South Yorkshire. However the makers of most of the blue glass mineral water bottles in this book are unknown as marked examples are the exception rather than the rule. Bottles such as the Hamilton in any colour of glass rarely have maker's marks, but a surprising number of other shapes in blue glass such as the cylinders are unmarked. Below are details of the few makers' names that do appear on blue glass bottles in this book.

A. Alexander & Company Blaydon

This firm, which also worked from Leeds, London and Sunderland, is well-known locally and 6oz and 10oz blue cylinders of W. B. Reid & Co. Ltd of Newcastle upon Tyne are known embossed with the abbreviated title of A. A. & Co. The 10oz blue codd of Robert Stephenson of Gateshead bears the firm's mark in full as A. ALEXANDER & CO/ MAKERS/ BLAYDON & LONDON.

A partnership trading as Alexander, Austin & Poole took over an existing bottle-works at Blaydon c.1861. The major partner, Alfred Alexander, was already making bottles at Hunslett in Leeds whilst John Battle Austin was a Sunderland shipbuilder and Henry Poole was the manager for the previous owners. The firm became Alexander & Austin by 1865 and bought a vacant bottle-works at Southwick in Sunderland. Around 1890 the firm became A. Alexander & Co. (*Development of the Glass Industry on the Rivers Tyne and Wear 1700-1900* Catherine Ross 1982 PhD thesis). The 1904 billhead from the firm shown below is from their Hunslett Glass Works branch at Leeds.

A. Alexander & Co. billhead 1904

Ayres Quay Bottle Co. Limited Sunderland

An example of a blue glass bottle with the well-known maker's mark of this major North East glass bottle-maker is an important recent find from 2010. Although only a partial example it is recognisable as a 6oz cylinder from Peter Thornton Limited of South Shields and the full maker's mark reads AYRES QUAY BOTTLE CO/ MAKERS/ SUNDERLAND.

The Ayres Quay Bottle Co. is celebrated in the North East for the wealth of superbly made and embossed beer, porter and mineral water bottles that it produced, many of which are among the finest in the area. Bottle making at Ayres Quay in Sunderland goes back as far as the late seventeenth century but the Ayres Quay Bottle Company that concerns us dates from 1820-1923 (*Glass Making on Wearside* Tyne & Wear County Council 1979 and The National Glass Centre Sunderland). The advertisement below is from Kelly's Post Office Directory of Durham for 1894.

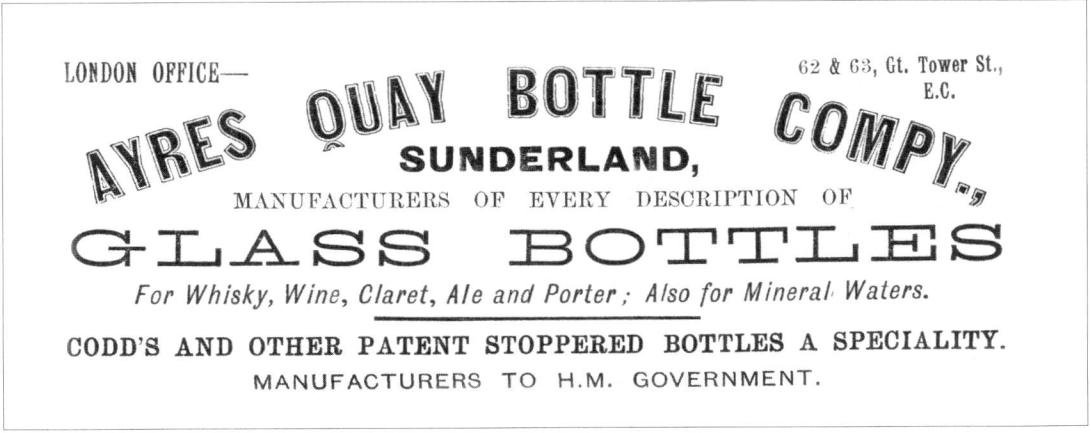

Ayres Quay Bottle Works advertisement 1894

Bagley & Co. Limited, Knottingley

A. Bagley & Co. Ltd advertisement 1909

This glassworks traded at Knottingley in Yorkshire and their mark, B & Co Ltd K, is found on the base of the blue champagne-shaped screw-stoppered bottle from William Robson of Sunderland.

The firm's title was Bagley, Wild & Co. (William Bagley, John William Bagley and John Wild) from 1871-1890 and Bagley & Co. from 1890-1898. The business was registered as a private company Bagley & Co. Ltd in June 1898 with William Bagley as chairman and managing director (Lockhart, Shriever, Serr, Lindsey and Gosney, Ron n.d.). The firm's advertisement shown is from the *Annual Report of the Northumberland & Durham Mineral Water and Ale & Porter Bottle Exchange Ltd* of 1909.

E. Breffit & Co. Limited

This maker's mark appears on the celebrated blue Codds of E. J. Stewart of West Hartlepool. The full mark reads E. BREFFIT & CO. LD./ MAKERS/ CASTLEFORD.

The firm was founded as Edgar Breffit & Co. before 1850 and was registered as a limited company on 12 March 1883 (*Grace's Guide to British Industrial History* 2007). The advertisement shown is from *The Mineral Water Trade Review and Guardian* February 1902 in the period that Stewart was ordering his blue glass Codd bottles from the firm.

E. Breffit & Co. Ltd advertisement 1902

Dobson & Nall Limited

This mark is seen on the celebrated Skittle Codd (flat-bottomed Codd-Hamilton hybrid) of Shimmin of Sunderland. The full mark reads DOBSON & NALL LTD/ BOTTLE/ & CASK MAKERS/ BARNSLEY.

Dobson & Nall Ltd traded from the Oaks Glass Bottle & Case Works at Barnsley which was founded in 1872 by T. Sutcliffe and C. Wade. John Dobson joined the partnership in 1877 and by 1884 was the sole owner. Between 1899 and 1903 he was joined by Jabez Nall to form the Dobson & Nall partnership (Mark Potten 2006). Nall's business as a case-maker had been wound up in 1902 (*Mineral Water Trade Review & Guardian* February 1902). The advertisement shown is from *The Mineral Water Trade Journal Supplement* October 1903, the same year that Shimmin ordered his hybrid blue Codd from the firm.

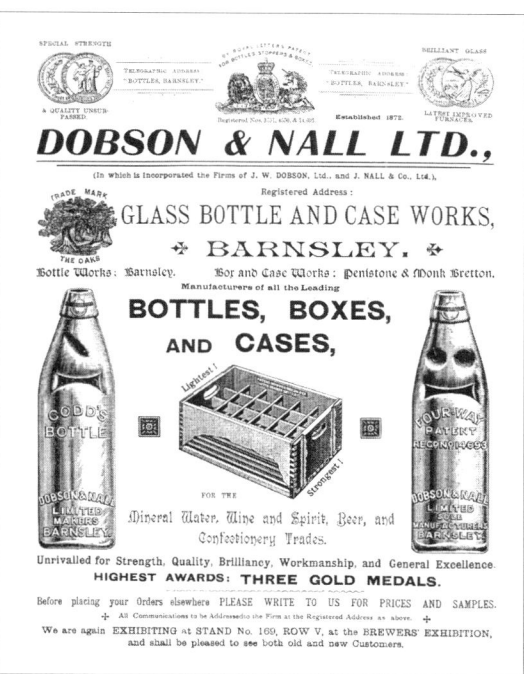

Dobson & Nall Ltd advertisement 1903

Redfearn Brothers, Barnsley

The mark of this well-known maker appears on the 10oz cylinder from W. B. Reid & Co. Ltd of Newcastle upon Tyne on which it consists of the abbreviated letters R B B.

The original works of this Yorkshire firm were on the site of the old corn mill of Barnsley which was converted to a glassworks in 1861. It was acquired in 1862 by Joshua and Samuel Redfearn, trading as Redfearn Brothers at the Old Mill Glassworks Barnsley. The firm took over further works at Wombwell in 1895 and survived through the twentieth century finally being bought by a Swedish firm in 1989 (Mark Potten 2006). The advertisement shown is from the *Mineral Water Trade Review & Guardian* December 1878.

Redfearn Brothers advertisement 1878

Dan Rylands, Barnsley

The North East catalogue has three blue glass bottles from this famous Barnsley bottle-maker; a Patent Safe Groove codd used by Emmerson Brothers of Newcastle, a 6oz cylinder from James Grieves & Sons of South Shields and the four-way patent from J. Kershaw & Sons of Gateshead.

The history of this firm at the Hope Glass Works, Stairfoot, Barnsley is at the core of the development of the mineral water bottle and will need little introduction to collectors. It was run by Ben Rylands (1874-77), Rylands & Codd (1877-81), Codd & Rylands (1882-84), Dan Rylands (1884-88) Dan Rylands Ltd (1888-97) and The Rylands Glass & Engineering Co. Ltd (1897-1927). These dates are from an article by Mark Potten in ABC magazine issue 51 of 2008. The billhead shown is from 1885.

Dan Rylands billhead 1885

CHAPTER 2

Shapes & Closures of Blue Glass Mineral Water Bottles

In the bottle-collecting hobby in the United Kingdom various names have come into usage to describe the shapes of mineral water bottles. Some of these have a claim to authenticity being contemporary nineteenth century terms but some are historically inaccurate. Added to these are terms which are used in the hobby in other countries some of which can also be found in use in the nineteenth century and some not. To avoid confusion I have continued to use the names that are in common usage today in the United Kingdom and have avoided terms such as egg-soda, ovate, egg-shape, torpedo and bowler whether they are historically more accurate or not. Examples of all the shapes described below will be found in the drawings of the bottles used by individual North East firms in chapter five.

Hamilton

This term, which is in general usage in our hobby, is accepted as not being historically accurate. It is used for a bottle which has an egg-shaped body with a pointed base which cannot be stood upright. The actual shape itself goes back at least to the early nineteenth century and was notably described by William Hamilton in his 1809 patent (no. 3232) for "A New Mode of Preparing Soda and other Mineral Waters..." in which he said that:

> I generally use a glass or earthen bottle of ovate form, for several reasons, viz, not having a square bottom to stand upon, it can only lie on its side, of course, no leakage of air can take place, the liquid matter being always in contact with the stopper. It can be much stronger than a bottle or jar of equal weight made in the usual form, and is therefore better adapted for packing, carriage etc.

The above quote outlines the two basic advantages of the shape of bottle described by William Hamilton, its innate strength and its efficiency in holding the internal pressure of its contents. A test for a glass-maker in the early twentieth century stated that "egg-ended soda water bottles" would stand the enormous pressure of 450lb per square inch before bursting, considerably more than the usual bottled pressure of around 60lb (*The Mineral Water Trade Journal* August 1906 and March 1913).

    A subsequent patent of William Hamilton in 1814 (no. 3819) for a carbonating machine included a drawing of his apparatus along with a bottle attached of a basic shape that we now call a Hamilton. William Hamilton himself described this bottle as "of ovate form" but did not patent the shape in either of his patents. In the mineral water trade press of the late nineteenth and early twentieth century the shape is commonly called an egg-soda, egg-shape or egg-ended soda. The bottle collecting hobby in the UK however named it after William Hamilton in the early 1970s and the name has stuck. The shape itself proved durable and Thomas Barron's Phoenix Glass Works in Mexborough Yorkshire for example was still advertising it among its range in the 1920s (*Mineral Water Trade Review & Guardian* 1922). The Hamilton is the commonest shape of blue glass mineral water bottle in the North East with over thirty different examples being recorded to date used by thirteen different firms.

Flat-bottomed Hamilton

This is a Hamilton in which the pointed end has been replaced with a flat base to enable the bottle to stand upright. It is known in two forms, one an elegant narrow shape and the other a broader bodied example. Although this shape loses the air-tight advantage of the Hamilton it does capitalise on the traditional and familiar Hamilton shape and the bottle could stand on its own without a special stand. Like the Hamilton shape itself it proved long-lasting and, along with the Hamilton, was also still being advertised by glass bottle makers in the 1920s (*Mineral Water Trade Review & Guardian* 1922). There are ten different types recorded at present used by six North East firms.

Cylinder

The cylinder shape was a popular one for mineral waters in the late nineteenth century. It has a long straight-sided body with a short neck and a flat base. *The Mineral Water Trade Review & Guardian* November 1878 summed up its popularity when it noted that:

> Although the egg-shaped bottle holds its ground, many mineral water manufacturers prefer the cylinder shape because the bottles pack closer together, and thus economise room and cost in cases, in consequence of which they are largely used for exporting ginger ale etc. It is a strong shape, and has a good appearance

It is the second commonest shape of blue glass mineral water bottle found in the North East with twenty two different examples recorded to date used by nine different firms.

Round-bottomed cylinder

This is a round-bottomed version of the cylinder described above. Like the Hamilton it has to be laid on its side and therefore has the same air-tight advantages of that bottle along with the packing advantages quoted above for the cylinder. It also needs a stand for use on the table. There are seven different types recorded used by five different firms.

Champagne shape

This was a very popular shape in the North East for a variety of bottles used for mineral waters, stout and ginger beer in both glass and stoneware. It has a straight-sided body with an indistinct shoulder leading into a long sloping neck, the body and neck each taking up about half the height of the bottle. There is only one example of this shape in the North East blue glass list which was used by William Robson of Sunderland.

Codd's patent bottle

This celebrated bottle with an internal closure using a glass marble was the brainchild of Hiram Codd who developed it in a series of patents starting with one dated 24 November 1870 (no. 3070). It was originally advertised as the "Globe-Stoppered Bottle" but is nowadays simply called the Codd after the name of its inventor. Four different North East firms are currently known to have used blue Codds with six different types so far recorded between them. The firms are E. J. Stewart of West Hartlepool (three standard Codds), Robert Stephenson of Gateshead (one standard Codd), Emmerson Brothers of Newcastle upon Tyne (one Patent Safe Groove Codd) and Shimmin of Sunderland (one Skittle-Codd). The Shimmin Codd is dealt with below as a separate shape.

Skittle-Codd (flat-bottomed Codd-Hamilton hybrid)

The celebrated blue Codd from George Shimmin of Sunderland is technically a flat-bottomed Codd-Hamilton hybrid (a Hamilton with a Codd's patent closure neck and a flat bottom) although this description is rather a mouthful and locally it has always been called a Skittle-Codd and I have continued to use this familiar name.

Four-way Patent

This is a champagne-shaped internal stopper with four dimples in the neck, no retaining cross-pinch and a double-ended glass bobbin stopper. It was patented by J. W. Dobson and was known as "Dobson's Four-Way Patent". The only blue example seen from a North East firm is however from J. Kershaw & Sons of Gateshead which has the maker's mark of Dan Rylands of Barnsley. It has exactly the same design and stopper as Dobson's more familiar bottle.

Ginger beer

This shape is traditionally accepted as a glass ginger beer and there is a blue glass example from J. Kershaw & Sons of Gateshead in the North East catalogue. It has a broad straight-sided body with a pronounced shoulder and a long neck. An article on bottle shapes being offered by the glass bottle-makers Kilner Brothers of Thornhill Lees in 1879 illustrates this shape and names it as a "ginger beer bottle" although the maker of Kershaw's bottle is unknown (*The Mineral Water Trade Recorder* 1 February 1879).

Blue glass bottle closures

The Hamilton, cylinder, round-bottomed cylinder and ginger beer shape all have conventional cork-stopper closures.

All the flat-bottomed Hamiltons also have cork-stopper closures except for Bradford Brothers of Newcastle upon Tyne type (3) which has an applied crown-cork closure.

The Codds all have aqua glass marble stoppers (where complete examples are known). The four-way patent from J. Kershaw & Sons of Gateshead has a double-ended glass bobbin stopper.

There is one standard internal screw-stopper in our blue glass catalogue which is the champagne-shaped blue mineral water bottle from William Robson of Sunderland. Credit for this closure is usually given to Henry Barrett of Hampton in Middlesex who patented it on 16 October 1879 (patent no. 4184) although this is more a reflection of his marketing expertise as various forms of internal screw-stoppers had been patented for some time before that date.

The crown-cork closure on the type (3) Bradford Brothers flat-bottomed Hamilton is the only example in our blue glass catalogue. It was invented by William Painter of Baltimore, Maryland in the USA and a patent was applied for it in the UK on 2 February 1892 (patent no. 2031) and accepted on 28 May. It has proved a durable closure still in use today. The term crown-cap is often used interchangeably for this closure.

Bottle lips

The majority of bottles in this book with cork-stopper closures had contents which were under significant pressure and their corks had to be wired securely onto the neck of the bottle. The anchor for the wire was provided by the lip of the bottle which was made of a thick applied ring of glass, the edges of which, in profile, are convex. They average around ¾ inch (19mm) in length and are known as blob-tops in the hobby. Typical blob-tops are seen on the Hamilton, the flat-bottomed Hamilton, the cylinder and the round-bottomed cylinder shapes.

A variation of this type of lip is known locally as the chisel-lip. It is essentially the same as the blob-top except that the ring of glass forming the lip has been flattened around its circumference so that in profile it appears straight-sided somewhat like the end of a chisel (hence the name). Chisel-lips vary in length from being only marginally longer than the conventional blob-top up to an elegant 1⅜ inches (35mm) in length. The longer examples, not surprisingly, are prone to damage and surviving examples seen today have sometimes been ground down and shortened to remove damage and make them more presentable. The longer chisel-lips are presumed to have been made to specific order to fit a buyer's particular filling machine.

The lip of the internal screw-thread closure seen on the champagne-shaped blue glass mineral water bottle of William Robson of Sunderland will be a familiar shape to collectors from its use on many different types of glass bottles in the late nineteenth and early twentieth century.

The ginger beer shape of J. Kershaw & Sons Gateshead also has a top used on many types of glass bottles in the same period. In essence it consists of a blob-top with a flared collar below it.

The lip of the crown-cork closure needs little introduction. Its shape has remained essentially unchanged until the present day and is illustrated on the Bradford Brothers of Newcastle upon Tyne flat-bottomed Hamilton type (3) in chapter five.

CHAPTER 3

Embossing, Etching and the A10 mark

Embossed bottles

In the early decades of the nineteenth century the embossing of bottles was achieved by having the metal moulds that bottles were blown in engraved on the inside with the required design. In the North East one famous source of this type of work was the Beilby-Bewick workshop in Newcastle, names now world famous for the enamelled glass developed by William and Mary Beilby (*The Ingenious Beilbys* 1973 and *A Beilby Odyssey* 1987 by James Rush) and the woodcarving done by the celebrated Thomas Bewick. The development of bottle-mould engraving in the nineteenth century at this workshop is well-covered in *The Tyne Glasshouses and Beilby-Bewick Workshop* by Margaret Ellison (Archaeologia Aeliana, series 5, vol. 3, 1975). Margaret Ellison notes that by 1830 the mould engraving had been largely superseded by the casting of moulds.

Etching

The term acid-etched is often used in the bottle collecting hobby to describe a design that has been etched onto the surface of glass bottles. The traditional method of etching glass is by the use of hydrofluoric acid but as a highly skilled and time-consuming process it was not a practical method for firms to use on bottles. A much cheaper and easier procedure for these was by sandblasting and this was promoted in the trade press as a means for marking bottles. We should, maybe, therefore use the term etched rather than acid-etched for our bottles.

Plain bottles were less expensive to buy than embossed bottles and so etching plain bottles by sandblasting was a cheaper alternative for mineral water manufacturers willing to invest in a sandblasting machine. Stencils of the required design would be placed over the bottle and high-pressure sand blasted at it would etch the stencil design onto the glass. The etched design appears whitish on any colour of glass and the method found some favour in the North East notably on black glass beer bottles where the resulting contrast of the etched design on a dense black background often gave a startlingly attractive result. By the same argument it should look stunning on cobalt blue glass but it appears not to have found the same favour here as there are only two etched blue glass mineral water bottles in the North East catalogue and both of them are very rare.

The article extract below promoting a cheap sand-blasting machine to mineral water manufacturers is from *The Mineral Water Trade Review and Guardian* April 1881.

A CHEAP SAND-BLAST FOR ENGRAVING BOTTLES

The advantage that would accrue to mineral water makers were they able to brand their bottles as required is almost obvious. Instead of having to purchase a great quantity of lettered bottles very early in the year, a large proportion of which lie as dead stock should the season turn out to be unpropitious, plain bottles could be purchased in quantities proportioned to the demand, and they could be washed and branded as wanted.

The principle of the sand-blast is that the forcible projection of a hard particle against an equally hard surface causes a scratch, or indentation, on the surface and if the process is repeated indefinitely the hard surface will be eventually cut through to any extent, just as if it had been done by a hammer and chisel.

In engraving on glass, very little pressure is needed, the current from the bellows of an enameller's lamp being quite sufficient. In this way, the divisions on graduated tubes, trade mark or names on bottles etc, can be easily engraved with but little trouble. The portions of glass which are to remain clear are covered with paper, or with an elastic varnish, these substances being sufficient protection against the abrading action of the sand.

The above article of 1881 did note that at the time numerous difficulties stood in the way of utilizing the well-known sand-blast process but suggested that the problems were capable of solution and showed a rather simple-looking device as an example. They were right however as by the end of the century more sophisticated machines were being advertised such as the one shown here from *The Pottery Gazette* of 1899 and many mineral water manufacturers and bottlers were using them.

Pottery Gazette advertisement December 1899

In the North East two etched blue glass Hamiltons are known. Both are from Newcastle, one from Gilpin & Co. and the other from James Mackie & Son. Hamiltons are normally embossed to be read lengthways but both of these etched examples are orientated to be read with the bottles upright. *A Descriptive Account of Newcastle, Illustrated* (c.1894) has a promotional article on Gilpin & Co. which specifically states that the firm used etched bottles:

> All bottles made for the firm have the name in full in raised letters, and those bought plain have the name of the firm stencilled by a special sand blast

In general etching on blue glass mineral water bottles did not find favour with the North East firms that used such bottles. This is underlined by the fact that several of the firms that used embossed blue mineral water bottles such as Bradford Brothers, W. Glendenning and William Row of Newcastle and Dowson Brothers of Gateshead are all known to have had sandblasting machines which they used on black beers and aqua mineral water bottles but no etched blue glass mineral waters are known from any of them.

Labelling

Most of the bottles in this book had to be labelled to show their contents. The only exceptions are the Hamiltons of George Eland of Newcastle (types 1, 2, 3, 4, 7, 8, 9) which actually have their contents named in the embossing as will be seen in chapter five. There were several companies in the North East supplying labels to the trade. John Christie of Newcastle was one such supplier and the advertisement of his shown is from *The Mineral Water Trade Review and Guardian* May 1877.

LABELS AND SHOW CARDS,
VARIETY OF SHAPES AND DESIGNS, SUITABLE FOR
MINERAL WATER MANUFACTURERS, PORTER AND SPIRIT MERCHANTS,
NEATLY LITHOGRAPHED BY
JOHN CHRISTIE, Caxton House, Newcastle-on-Tyne.
SAMPLES AND PRICES ON APPLICATION.

John Christie advertisement May 1877

The A10 mark (Alliance Number)

This very familiar mark seen on glass and stoneware bottles from the North East is a useful means of dating items. During the last quarter of the nineteenth century local mineral water trade associations were formed throughout the country to monitor and protect the interests of their members. The one for the North East had the unwieldy title of the Northumberland & Durham Mineral Water and Ale and Porter Bottle Exchange and Trade Protection Society Limited. Its activities included the running of bottle-exchanges which were sorting houses for ensuring that embossed and etched bottles could be returned to the right firms. These associations had an overall governing body known as the Alliance of Mineral Water Manufacturers' Associations Limited. By the 1890s the loss of bottles to businesses was proving such a serious matter for mineral water manufacturers that an effort was made by the Alliance to reduce it. In October 1891 the Alliance held a meeting to discuss the problem and its suggested course of action was to introduce a nationwide system of marking bottles. This was reported in *The Mineral Water Trade Recorder* December 1891 as shown below. The report included a copy of a letter that had already been sent out in September to all the branches of the Alliance.

The Alliance

A meeting of the Directors of the Alliance took place recently....A scheme by which bottles belonging to remote districts can be more easily identified was considered, and the Secretary reported that the majority of replies to the following letter were in favour of the numbering process:-

The Alliance of Mineral Water Manufacturers' Association Limited
Registered Office: Call, Leeds
September 12th 1891

Dear Sir,

The attention of the Alliance Directors has been called to the difficulty frequently experienced by the sorters employed by the various associations in identifying bottles belonging to the members in outside or comparatively unknown places... With the object, therefore, of assisting sorters in all parts of the kingdom to identify any stray bottles, and so facilitate their return to their rightful owners, the directors propose to give what may be termed an "Alliance Number", or other distinguishing mark, to every existing association, so that members of any society who reside in a remote or comparatively unknown place can, by having the Alliance number or mark placed on their bottles...ensure their return from any part of the kingdom.

Below are the names of the societies in England and two proposed methods of marking, and I shall be glad if you will inform me which you prefer, or if neither, send any suggestion that you think is better.

Birmingham	A1 or B1
Bolton	A2 or B0
Devon and Cornwall	A4 or D&C

Isle of Wight	A5 or IoW
Kent	A6 or K
Liverpool	A7 or L
London	A8 or LO
Manchester	A9 or M
Northumberland	A10 or ND
Nottingham	A11 or NM
North Stafford	A12 or NS
Portsmouth	A13 or P
Wigan	A14 or W
Yorkshire	A15 or Y

When the directors decide at their next meeting in October which method is best, bills will be printed, in large type, and a quantity forwarded to the secretary of each respective association, who will supply their sorters with a copy, to be posted up in the bottle exchanges, and when all bottles bear the Alliance number or mark the advantage will be that sorters will have only a few numbers or marks to deal with instead of innumerable towns and places...if all members of associations...when ordering new bottles, have the Alliance number or mark of the their respective association plainly imprinted in the glass there will be no difficulty...of identifying them and returning them to the association to which they belong.

I shall be glad to hear from you on this subject at your earliest convenience.

I am dear sir, yours faithfully,

W. Tooke, Secretary

The numbering process was adopted.

This numbering system of marking bottles was adopted at the October 1891 meeting and all further new bottles of members were to be marked with their appropriate Alliance number. Under this system the North East association (shortened to Northumberland in the letter above but including Durham) was allocated the Alliance Number 10 which we know as the **A10** mark. Had the vote gone the other way and the letters system adopted our bottles would have had ND on the base instead of A10. For dating purposes therefore bottles bearing the A10 mark must be post-1891.

CHAPTER 4

Restoration and Polishing

Before moving on to the details of the bottles and the North East firms that used them some words about the restoration of blue glass mineral water bottles are appropriate. This is relevant as the increasing availability in recent times of restoration, in particular acid-polishing and tumbling, has had questionable results on a significant number of the surviving examples of such bottles.

Attempts to physically rebuild damaged blue glass mineral water bottles rarely achieve reasonable results as I think most collectors would agree. Whilst the replacement of small chips in a deep blue example can be done with a degree of success by a talented restorer, in general the results of rebuilding large missing sections or the attachment of new tops to incomplete examples are nearly always visually unattractive. In the case of Codd bottles, particularly in deep blue glass, the professional attachment of a new top can produce an acceptable result and is a means of enabling the collector to have an example of a very rare or even unique bottle especially given the price that complete examples now fetch.

Most of the blue glass mineral water bottles that we are concerned with come from ash-tips where they ended up among the ash and general rubbish over a century ago. As collectors will be aware the burial of glass bottles in damp alkaline ash often results in the soda and lime in the glass being attacked over time leaving a white film of silica on the glass surface. The resulting frosted appearance, very familiar to diggers and collectors, has long been given the name sickness which, in an advanced state, can be iridescent. Cellar and attic found blue glass mineral water bottles do exist and I remember the first such one that I ever saw which was in the 1970s and was an immaculate 6oz flat-bottomed hamilton from Bradford Brothers of Newcastle upon Tyne. Sadly these are the exception rather than the rule and most surviving examples have been dug.

Diggers and collectors will be well aware of how to clean dug bottles including removing rust deposits and they will also know that sickness on glass bottles cannot be removed by conventional cleaning methods. In the 1970s one early NDBCC member was adept at slowly and carefully polishing off small areas of sickness on blue glass bottles using jewellers rouge (cerium oxide). However this needs skill and an enormous amount of patience and is not a practical method for most of us.

Using powerful acids to get rid of sickness by removing a layer of glass from the surface of the bottle was first noted by a chemist, Clifford Green, in his book *Cleaning*

Methods, A Dump Diggers Guide (Southern Collectors Publications Southampton 1977). Understandably he did not give details of the very toxic acids and dangerous processes involved and cautioned against any amateur attempting it. This procedure is known as acid-polishing.

The other method of getting rid of sickness is by tumbling. In use in the USA for many years for polishing bottles this process was a natural extension of its use in polishing stones for jewellery purposes. It is a much cleaner process as it does not involve the use of acids and works by rotating the bottle in a machine over a period of time in various grades of polishing grit and water which will gradually polish off the surface layer of the bottle.

Both processes have been available commercially in the UK for some time now, acid-polishing longer than tumbling, and the end result of both is the permanent removal of a layer of glass from the bottle surface. As well as the safety aspects they both need a fair degree of skill and empathy in the operator in trying to achieve the minimal alteration to the appearance of the bottle. Some of the blue glass mineral waters we are concerned with here are quite finely embossed to start with and can suffer disproportionately when attempts are made to polish them. Unfortunately polishing does not restore bottles to the state they were in when they left the bottle-makers. It leaves a bright but warm and soft-looking finish to the glass that differs significantly to the cold diamond-hard look seen on original items.

When acid-polishing became generally available in the 1990s it became increasingly popular to have glass bottles polished, particularly coloured glass examples, and as a consequence examples in original condition have become increasingly rare. There was a tendency to go for the removal of not only sickness but even the slight scuffs and marks that occur on the majority of dug bottles. Certainly since the millennium many blue glass mineral water bottles on the market have been irreversibly changed by over-polishing; a bright sparkling finish having been achieved at the expense of radically reducing the embossing. Blue glass mineral water bottles are not common nor are they likely to become so. They are a limited resource and it is sad to see examples permanently altered, even ruined, by such efforts.

There is no easy answer to the question of condition as the appearance of any glass bottle is very much a matter of taste. Attractive iridescence on a shaft and globe wine bottle for example would actually be valued rather than the reverse and there would be no question of having it polished off. However I'd be the first to admit that very sick blue glass mineral water bottles can look pretty unattractive and a light polishing by a skilled and sympathetic operator would be accepted by most collectors as the lesser of two evils in such cases. Personally I accept signs of wear and tear and even some sickness on an otherwise original condition bottle rather than have a whole bottle polished just to get a bright finish. An added consideration here is that there is a degree of risk in both polishing processes, albeit small, but breakages have been known to occur.

These days the term "cleaning" is being used more and more, both here and in the USA, almost as a euphemism for acid-polishing and tumbling both of which I consider as forms of restoration; cleaning is done with soap and water! Polished bottles should be regarded and valued as restored items and in the long-term they will certainly be considered as such, as do all antiques, when compared to untouched examples.

Think before you polish is my maxim and if you do decide to go down that line then look around, there are polishers out there who have empathy for bottles and will do a sympathetic job.

CHAPTER 5

The North East Firms and their Blue Glass Mineral Water Bottles

This chapter covers, in alphabetical order, the firms in the North East which are known to have used blue glass mineral water bottles. The types of bottles known from each firm are described and illustrated along with a summarised history of each business, under the heading Notes, taken from trade directories, the mineral water trade press, promotional books, census returns and newspapers.

John Arkle, Morpeth

(1) 6oz Hamilton
(2) 10oz Hamilton

Our first blue glass mineral water bottles are the Hamiltons used by John Arkle of the Northumberland market town of Morpeth. With their trade mark of George and the Dragon they are among the most desirable bottles in blue glass from the North East. Until 1990 only a single 6oz example was known to exist but in that year a 10oz example and three more 6oz examples appeared together having been dug, it was said, from one site many years previously. The story of their appearance is worth repeating. A slightly blurred photograph of the said four blue Hamiltons displayed on a front room windowsill was published, with permission, in the *NDBCC newsletter no. 47 (1989)*. Despite total anonymity the location was tracked down by club members, from the view outside of the front room window it was said, and the bottles came onto the market. Bottle sleuthing at its finest! I am not aware of any further whole examples being found since then.

    The George & Dragon Yard in Morpeth was one of a series of yards in the town which developed from medieval land strips. Maps show that it was a long narrow alley behind the George & Dragon Inn which ran from the Market Place down to the river Wansbeck the many buildings down both sides consisting of tenements and a wide variety of businesses (*The Curious Yards & Alleyways of Morpeth*: Bridget Gubbins, Morpeth 2011).

    The 6oz and 10oz size Hamiltons both have conventional blob-tops for cork-stoppers. They have the same open embossed design on one side of the bottle which consists of the firm's trade mark of St. George on horseback killing the dragon with the words **John Arkle** above and **Morpeth** below. They should date to c.1884-85 as discussed in the notes below. The 6oz Hamilton is illustrated.

John Arkle 6oz Hamilton

Notes:

a) Relevant trade directory listings of the Arkle family in Morpeth are as follows:
    - 1868-1884 John Arkle, coal lime and manure agent, cart owner, Chantry Place
    - 1884 Thomas Arkle, aerated water manufacturer, George & Dragon yard
    - 1886 Margaret Arkle, aerated water manufacturer, George & Dragon yard
    - 1890-1894 Margaret Arkle, coal, lime & manure agent, Chantry Place & Station

b) The letter-head from John Arkle shown, dated 3 May 1878, shows that he was then an agent for Cowpen Colliery and was working from the Blyth and Tyne Coal Depot at Morpeth Station. Written to a W. Dickson, the presumed site owner, its contents relate to a boundary dispute with the Morpeth committee. The letter is signed by John Arkle.

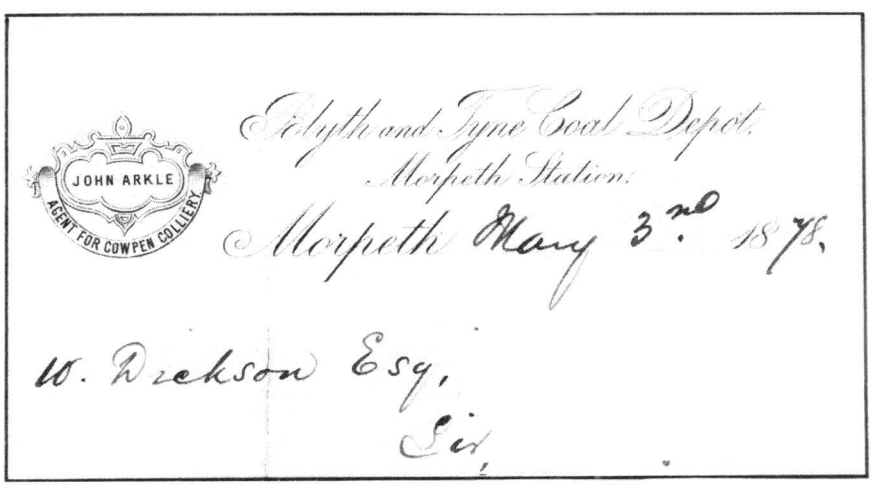

John Arkle letter-head of 3 May 1878

c) Census returns record (with ages in brackets) that in 1861 a John Arkle (39), coal agent, born at Rothbury Northumberland, was living at Chantry Place Morpeth with his wife Margaret (48), born in Alnwick, and their children Eleanor (10), Thomas (8) and Margaret (6). In 1871, still a coal agent, he was living with his family at High Church Cottage, Morpeth Castle. In 1881 they also had a live-in servant Elizabeth Green. John Arkle died at Morpeth, in December 1885 aged 65 and Thomas Arkle died at Morpeth, in March 1890 aged 37.

d) *The Mineral Water Trade Review & Guardian* July 1885 contained the following interesting report ("Mr Akers" is a misprint for Mr Arkle and refers to John Arkle and his son Thomas Arkle):

Mr. Akers of Morpeth, is carrying on business as a mineral water manufacturer, which a short time ago he started for his son. He is fortunate in the possession of an almost inexhaustible spring of the purest crystal water which, according to an analysis by a gentleman well qualified to give an opinion, is pre-eminently suited for the purposes for which it is now being applied. There is many a firm who would give a large sum of money for such a spring, and I shall confidently expect to hear of some good results in time to come.

e) John Arkle himself is not recorded as a mineral water manufacturer but the directory, census and trade press reports above suggest that he started the aerated water business (presumably under his own name) as a sideline to his coal agency on behalf of his son Thomas in 1884 or early 1885. He died in December 1885 after which Thomas continued the business until 1886 when his mother, Margaret assumed control. Rare internally stopped aqua bottles are known from both Thomas Arkle and Margaret Arkle suggesting that the blue Hamiltons of John Arkle should date to the earlier days of the firm circa 1884-85. The coal, lime and manure agency appears to have been a bread and butter trade of the Arkle family in the late nineteenth century which is less romantic than the blue George and the Dragon Hamiltons would suggest but they are no less collectable for that.

f) The George and the Dragon trade mark is also known on rare black glass ginger beer bottles from a firm titled Bell & Black, Morpeth which does not appear in directory listings. The Bell is probably a William Bell who is listed as manager for Margaret Arkle in 1886. In 1897 the firm of Forsyth & Thompson, mineral water manufacturer, is listed in the George & Dragon yard.

* * *

John J. Bell, Newcastle upon Tyne

(1) 10oz Hamilton

J. J. Bell is one of the lesser known mineral water manufacturers from Newcastle and I have only ever seen the one, incomplete, example of their 10oz blue Hamilton as illustrated which was brought into an NDBCC meeting in 1986. It is embossed on one side **John J. Bell** and **Newcastle on Tyne** and on the other **Genuine Superior** and **Aerated Water**. The style of lip is unknown although a complete aqua version of this bottle is known which has a conventional blob-top for a cork-stopper. The firm is also known to have used aqua glass mineral water bottles, including Hamiltons, with the firm's registered trade mark of a bell prominently embossed, including examples with the embossing laid out in the outline of a bell, however there is no evidence that these were made in blue glass. From the firm's history outlined below this blue Hamilton should date to the 1869-70 period when the firm's title was John James Bell. Both sides of the known incomplete example of the 10oz Hamilton are illustrated.

J. J. Bell 10oz Hamilton

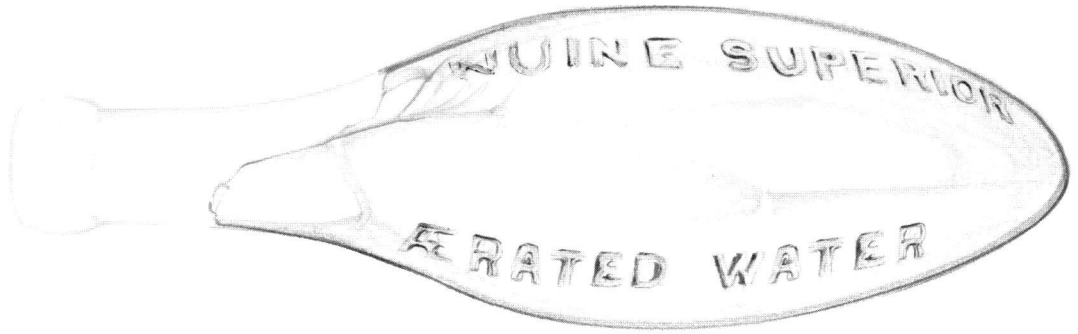

J. J. Bell 10oz Hamilton reverse

Notes:

a) The firm appears under three titles at Newcastle upon Tyne:
- 1869-1870 John James Bell, ale & porter merchant, importer & manufacturer of mineral waters, 7 Manor Chare
- 1870-1872 Bell, Routledge & Co., ale, porter wine & ice merchants, importer & manufacturer of mineral waters, 7 Manor Chare
- 1873-1879 J. J. Bell & Co., mineral water manufacturer, ale stout and ice merchant importer of wine and natural mineral waters etc., Forth Street and South Street

b) The advertisement shown from Ward's Directory of Newcastle etc. 1869-70 notes that J. J. Bell had previously spent nine years with Gilpin & Company, one of Newcastle's oldest mineral water manufacturers, and one that also used blue glass mineral water bottles (q.v.).

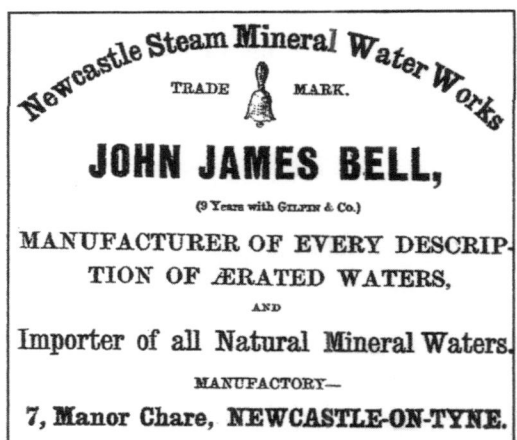

Advertisement from Ward's Directory of Newcastle 1869-70

c) *The London Gazette* of 5 March 1872 announced the liquidation of Bell, Routledge & Company noting that creditors of John James Bell were required on or before 8 March to send their details to Thomas Strachan, Grainger Street West, Newcastle upon Tyne, the trustee under the liquidation.

d) J. J. Bell & Co. applied to register a depiction of a bell as a trade mark on 13 March 1876 in Class 44 (no. 3797) for mineral and aerated waters claiming its use from 2 years before that date. It was registered on 30 August 1876 and has only been seen on aqua mineral water bottles from the firm.

e) *The Mineral Water Trade Review and Guardian* May 1879 announced that Richard Wightman, mineral water manufacturer, of Newcastle upon Tyne had bought J. J. Bell & Co.'s business at Forth Street Newcastle having purchased it as "a going concern from the liquidators of Mr Bell's estate". It also says, somewhat waspishly, that "this business has passed through various vicissitudes of misfortune" and noted that if the late proprietor had devoted as much attention to the firm's economics as he had to outside matters the outcome might have been quite different!

f) An announcement of the liquidation of the business of John James Bell & Co. appeared in *The Mineral Water Trade Review and Guardian* February 1881.

g) From 1881 J. J. Bell is listed solely as an agent for various national brewers and distillers at offices in South Street and then Pink Lane in Newcastle. A short promotional article on his agency business appears in *Tyneside Industries* (1889).

h) In summary the above details suggest that J. J. Bell started a mineral water business on his own in Newcastle in 1869 after spending nine years learning the trade at Gilpin & Co. in the town. By 1870 he had a partner called Routledge who is not listed by name otherwise in Newcastle. In early 1872 the partnership of Bell, Routledge & Co. was liquidated and the following year saw J. J. Bell Co. as a mineral water manufacturer and ale & porter merchant at Forth Street Newcastle. J. J. Bell & Co was liquidated in 1879 and Richard Wightman acquired the Forth Street business after which J. J. Bell is listed only as a commission agent.

* * *

Bewick Brothers, Blaydon

(1) 6oz Hamilton
(2) 10oz Hamilton

Bewick Brothers is the only firm from the Tyneside township of Blaydon known to have used blue glass mineral water bottles. The firm is well-known to collectors from its attractive trade mark of two deer which it used on most of its glass and stoneware bottles. Among its mineral waters are 6oz and 10oz blue glass Hamiltons both of which are rare and highly sought-after. They have conventional blob-tops for cork-stoppers and are embossed on one side of the bottle as shown. The detailed open design has the words **Bewick Bros** at the top and **Blaydon** at the bottom with the trade mark of two deer between them with **Registered** above it and **Trade Mark** and the registration number **No. 74599** below. It's a striking design but is usually not very well embossed on either size. The 10oz Hamilton is illustrated.

Notes:

a) Bewick Brothers worked from a mineral water manufactory on Church Street, Blaydon which is listed under the following firms:
- 1871-1877 Joseph Makepeace, mineral water manufacturer, ale & porter merchant
- 1877-1880 Joseph Makepeace & Son, mineral water maker, ale & porter merchant

Bewick Brothers 10oz Hamilton

- 1881-1884 M. Makepeace & Co., mineral water manufacturer
- 1885-1888 Thompson & Bewick, ale & porter merchant
- 1888-1909 Bewick Brothers, mineral water manufacturer, ale & porter merchant
- 1910-1925 Fields Brothers, mineral water manufacturer, ale & porter merchant

No blue glass mineral water bottles are known from any of the other firms at this manufactory.

b)   Joseph Makepeace, who founded the business, is listed as a stationer at Wesley Place, Blaydon 1855-1876. His son was also called Joseph and the firm is named as Joseph Makepeace & Son in a testimonial dated March 1877 for Codd's Patent in *The Mineral Water Trade Review & Guardian* July 1877. The same trade paper in December 1881 recorded the dissolution of the partnership of "Makepeace & Co., Blaydon, lemonade manufacturers and ale and porter merchants November 30th 1881. Debts by James Jenkins."

c)   The partners of Thompson & Bewick are listed as William Thompson, John Bewick and Luke Bewick.

d)   The proprietors of Bewick Brothers are listed as:
  - 1888-1902 John and Luke Bewick
  - 1903-1904 Luke Bewick
  - 1905-1909 William & Luke Bewick

e)   The trade mark of two deer appearing on the firm's blue Hamiltons was first used by Thompson & Bewick although it was Luke Bewick, acting for Bewick Brothers, who applied to register it as a trade mark in Class 44 (no. 74,599) for mineral and aerated waters on 3 April 1888.

f) The firm of Bewick Brothers was a member of the Northumberland & Durham Mineral Water and Ale & Porter Bottle Trade Protection Society Ltd being mentioned in the company's reports in the mineral water trade press in 1892 and 1907. The firm joined with other mineral water manufacturers in 1892 in an unsuccessful attempt to form the Northern Bottle Manufacturing Co. Ltd (*NDBCC newsletter* no. 95).

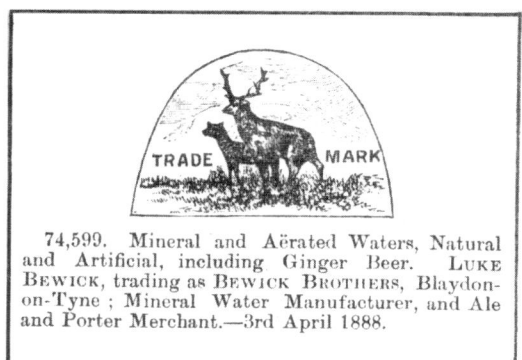

Trade mark registration of Bewick Brothers

g) *The Mineral Water Trade Journal* August 1909 reported the death of Luke Bewick of Bewick Brothers at the age of 64 who "had been in failing health for some time and was found dead in bed". He was interred in Blaydon Cemetery. The same journal in April 1910 reported his estate as having been proved at £3,168.

Advertisement from a promotional 1906 calendar

* * *

F. Bradford, Newcastle

(1) 6oz Hamilton
(2) 10oz Hamilton
(3) 6oz flat-bottomed Hamilton
(4) 10oz flat-bottomed Hamilton

With the distinctive trade mark of three fish the rare blue glass mineral water bottles of F. Bradford of Newcastle are among the most sought-after from the North East. All four types have the same embossed design on one side of the bottle which consists of the firm's name **F. Bradford** and **Newcastle** between which is the firm's trade mark of a representation of three fish within a circle (possibly representing a plate) with the words **Trade** and **Mark**. The bases of types (3) and (4), the flat-bottomed Hamiltons, are plain. Francis Lough Bradford was initially a partner in Bradford Brothers of Newcastle upon Tyne, a long-running mineral water manufacturing business that also used blue glass mineral water bottles (see notes below). The 10oz Hamilton and the 10oz flat-bottomed Hamilton are both illustrated.

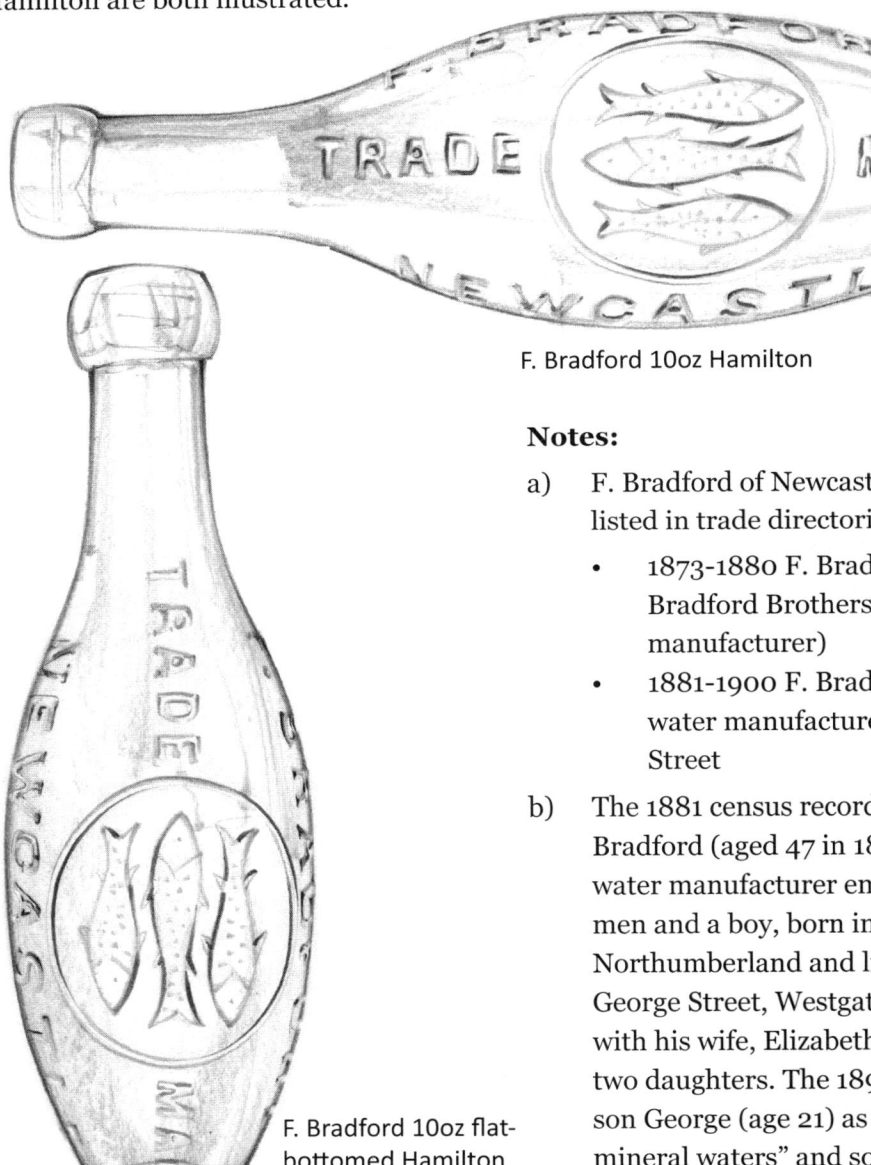

F. Bradford 10oz Hamilton

F. Bradford 10oz flat-bottomed Hamilton

Notes:

a) F. Bradford of Newcastle upon Tyne is listed in trade directories:
- 1873-1880 F. Bradford (of Bradford Brothers mineral water manufacturer)
- 1881-1900 F. Bradford, mineral water manufacturer, 12 Churchill Street

b) The 1881 census records Francis Bradford (aged 47 in 1881), mineral water manufacturer employing four men and a boy, born in Warkworth Northumberland and living at 15 George Street, Westgate, Newcastle with his wife, Elizabeth, four sons and two daughters. The 1891 census has son George (age 21) as a "traveller for mineral waters" and son Francis (age

19) a "bottler of mineral waters". Both are mentioned in the bankruptcy hearing below.

c) The directory listings record that Francis and George Bradford were the partners in Bradford Brothers until 1881 at which time Francis Bradford started a business under his own name leaving George Bradford as the sole partner in Bradford Brothers. This is at odds with what was reported in Francis Bradford's bankruptcy hearing below in which he suggested that he left Bradford Brothers around 1893. However an announcement in *The Mineral Water Trade Review & Guardian Supplement* January 1880 records the partnership dissolution of "Bradford Brothers, Newcastle, soda water manufacturers. Debts by G. Bradford." This supports the trade directory listings and would appear to be the actual date that Francis Bradford left Bradford Brothers (see also Bradford Brothers below).

d) Francis Lough Bradford of 15 George Street and 1 Churchill Street Newcastle had a petition for bankruptcy at Newcastle Bankruptcy Court dated 20 August 1900 and a first public hearing on 20 September 1900. The *Aerator & Bottler* October 1900 reported the public examination of Francis Lough Bradford at Newcastle Bankruptcy Court:

At the Newcastle Bankruptcy Court, Francis Lough Bradford, aerator, was publically examined. The debtor stated that he was first a partner in the firm of Bradford Brothers and when that firm was dissolved seven years ago he received the sum of £1,700 from his brother. The money was paid £500 down and £200 per annum for six years. He commenced in the same business on his own account after that, and took an active interest in it until latterly, when failing health kept him mainly at home. Since then his sons, Francis and George, managed the affairs and took their wages at discretion. He himself received about £2 per week from the business. His sons were not partners, though he believed that four years ago the title of the firm was altered to Francis Bradford & Sons without his actual knowledge. His son John James received some property at Amble through the will of a sister lately deceased, but any statement made by the other sons as to that property being available for the firm's debts was not made with his (debtor's) knowledge. The Official Receiver – "How do you explain your son John James being returned as a creditor for the sum of £290?" – "He mortgaged one of his houses in order to pay the firm's debts". "Can you explain how such an old-established firm as yours came to grief over the sum of £900?" – "It is owing to the great brewing syndicates having launched out in that line. The firm has been feeling the effect of the syndicates for the past eight or ten years". Examination adjourned.

e) His premises at 12 Churchill Street were taken over by Duncan & Daglish Ltd, brewer, wine & spirit merchant, licensed victualler and mineral water manufacturer.

f) The device of three fish was a popular trade mark and no record was found in the *Trade Mark Journals* of an application by F. Bradford to register it.

* * *

Bradford Brothers, Newcastle

(1) 6oz flat-bottomed Hamilton
(2) 10oz flat-bottomed Hamilton
(3) 10oz flat-bottomed crown-cap Hamilton

The bottles of Bradford Brothers, a mineral water manufacturer, ale & porter merchant, and restaurant & hotel proprietor in Newcastle upon Tyne are well-known to local collectors. The firm used an attractive trade mark of a stag's head which is seen on all three types of blue glass flat-bottomed Hamiltons known from the firm.

Types (1) and (2) have conventional blob-tops for cork-stoppers and my own 6oz example was the first blue that I purchased several decades ago for the princely sum of £25. Both types have the same open embossed design on one side of the bottle which consists of the firm's name **Bradford Bros** and **Newcastle** with the firm's trade mark of a stag's head between them along with the words **Registered** and **Trade Mark** as shown. The bases are plain.

Type (3), another 10oz flat-bottomed Hamilton, has a neat applied crown-cap. The bottle has a broader body and base and although not as elegant it is a more stable shape than types (1) and (2). The embossing is the same design seen on the first two types but it lacks the word **Registered** above the trade mark. The base has the letter **A** embossed on it and measures 1⅞ inches (47mm) across compared to 1¼ inches (32mm) for the base of the comparable type (2) and it holds 13oz to the brim compared to the 10oz that type (2) holds brimful. Although a crown-cap on a blue Hamilton may sound somewhat incongruous I still find this an attractive bottle and it is rare. The 6oz flat-bottomed Hamilton and the 10oz flat-bottomed crown-cap Hamilton are illustrated.

Notes:
a) Trade directories list Bradford Brothers in Newcastle upon Tyne as follows:
   - 1873-1874 Bradford Brothers, Brunel Street
   - 1875-1884 Bradford Brothers, Payne's Yard, Leazes Lane
   - 1885-1934 Bradford Brothers, 22 & 24 Elswick East Terrace

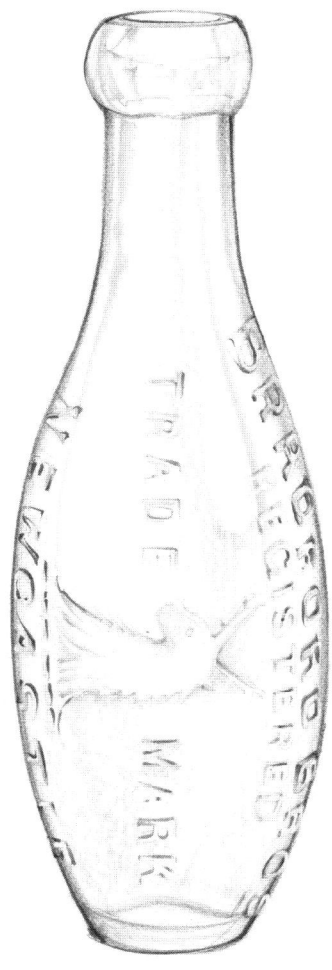

Bradford Bros. 6oz flat-bottomed Hamilton

Bradford Bros. 10oz flat-bottomed crown-cap Hamilton

- 1913-1920 Bradford Brothers, Collingwood Restaurant, 7 Groat Market
- 1916-1933 Bradford Brothers, 10 Rutherford Street
- 1926-1934 Bradford Brothers, Carlton Hotel, 6 Cloth Market

The firm is listed as a mineral water manufacturer at the Brunel Street, Payne's Yard and Elswick East Terrace addresses, as an ale & porter merchant at Elswick East Terrace from 1881, as a restaurant & hotel proprietor at the Collingwood Restaurant and the Carlton Hotel and as a motor car dealer, repairer and haulage contractor at 10 Rutherford Street. The firm is also listed as a motor car dealer at 3 St Nicholas's buildings in 1922.

b) The Elswick East Terrace address is listed under the Newcastle Cooperative Bakery from 1935. The Collingwood Restaurant is listed under Trust House Ltd by 1925 and the Carlton Hotel is listed under the Edinburgh brewers Steel, Coulson & Co. Ltd in 1924.

c) Proprietors of the firm are listed as:
- 1873-1880 Francis and George Bradford
- 1882-1903 George Bradford
- 1904-1907 Mrs George Bradford
- 1908-1920 Fred and Herbert Bradford
- 1921 Mrs F. E. Bradford and Fred Bradford
- 1922-1933 Fred Bradford

For Francis Bradford's part in the firm see the notes above under F. Bradford. Fred Bradford may have worked for the firm before 1908 as he is listed as a mineral water manufacturer at his home address from 1895.

d) *The Mineral Water Trade Review & Guardian Supplement* January 1880 reported, under partnership dissolutions, that of "Bradford Brothers, Newcastle, soda water manufacturers. Debts by G. Bradford."

e) The 1881 census records a George Bradford (aged 40), an ale & porter merchant born at Low Buston Northumberland and living at 32 Simpson Street Newcastle with his wife, Alice, and two daughters, a son, a brother-in-law and a general servant. The same year a William John Bradford (aged 42) at 229 Hamilton Street is noted as foreman in a soda water manufacturer's firm with a son Roger Bradford as a "waggonman" and a William John Bradford (junior) a labourer both for a soda water manufacturer.

BRADFORD BROTHERS,
ALE AND PORTER MERCHANTS,
AND
AERATED WATER MANUFACTURERS,
ELSWICK EAST TERRACE
(LATE OF LEAZES LANE),
NEWCASTLE-ON-TYNE. (8)

Advertisement from Kelly's Directory of Northumberland 1890

f) The stag's head trade mark used by the firm was a popular design and no application by Bradford Brothers to register it was found in the *Trade Mark Journals* despite the use of the word Registered in the embossing on types (1) and (2).

* * *

Crystal Aerated Water Co., Newcastle

(1) 10oz Hamilton

The first example of the 10oz blue Hamilton from the Crystal Aerated Water Co. of Newcastle upon Tyne that I saw was in the 1980s and it is still a rare bottle. No other types of blue glass bottles are known from the firm.

It has a conventional blob-top for a cork-stopper and is embossed on one side of the bottle with the words **Crystal Aerated/ Water Co/ Newcastle** as shown. The embossing does not note the firm as a limited company which should date the bottle to the 1890-1902 period as detailed in the notes below.

Crystal Aerated Water Co. 10oz Hamilton

Notes:
a) The firm is listed as a mineral water manufacturer and ale & stout bottler at:
   - 1890-1926 Temple Street, Newcastle upon Tyne
   - 1891-1897 27 Newgate Street, Newcastle upon Tyne
   - 1903-1926 West Blandford Street, Newcastle upon Tyne
b) There is a possible connection with an earlier similarly titled firm. *The Mineral Water Trade Review & Guardian* July 1885 reported that:

> There is a new firm started who have taken up quarters in Gallowgate, Newcastle, and are trading under the suggestive title The Crystal Co. It would appear that this company is not a "limited" one, and is composed mainly, if not entirely, of publicans resident in the town and district, with Mr. Rolf (brewer's agent) secretary and manager.

Bottles are known embossed with the name Crystal Water Co. (Robertson 2012) which is a firm listed at Back Lane, off Gallowgate, Newcastle 1887-1889. In 1890, the year after its disappearance, the similarly titled Crystal Aerated Water Co. appears at Temple Street (a different location). The possible connecting factor between the two firms is Charles Henry Rowland Rolf, the man noted in the 1885 trade press announcement to be the manager of the Crystal Water Co. From 1887 he is listed as an agent at 27 Newgate Street which is the same address listed for the Crystal Aerated Water Co. from 1891 suggesting his possible involvement with both companies.

c) The firm is listed as the Crystal Aerated Water Co. Ltd from 1902.

d) The manufactory address is given as Temple Street 1890-1901 and as 11 Blenheim Street from 1902-1908. The street listings suggest that both are correct and that the manufactory was on a corner site.

e) The Newgate Street address is listed as offices in Albion Chambers which also housed offices of some of Newcastle's wine and spirit merchants and several Scottish and Burton brewers.

f) The West Blandford Street address is likewise listed as offices variously numbered 10-20, 20 or 18. These numbers also housed offices of local and Scottish brewers.

g) In 1927 the firm Archibald Tower & Co. Ltd, mineral water manufacturer, is listed at the Temple Street premises.

* * *

James Deuchar, Newcastle

(1) 10oz Hamilton

An example of this rare 10oz blue Hamilton from the well-known firm of James Deuchar was first seen in the local hobby as late as 2004. It has a conventional blob-top for a cork-stopper and is embossed **J. Deuchar/ 199 Pilgrim St/ Newcastle** on one side of the bottle as shown. As the notes below show this Pilgrim Street address was the Ridley Arms Yard Brewery and dates the bottle to 1879-1893. No other examples of blue glass are known embossed with the Deuchar name on them although he did use a flat-bottomed blue Hamilton under the name of Ross & Co. Newcastle which is dealt with later in this chapter.

James Deuchar 10oz Hamilton

Notes:

a) James Deuchar was a giant in the brewing and bottling industry of the North East and a brief summary of the history of his business is given below. The information is taken from contemporary trade directories and the mineral water trade press although it should be said that some history sources differ at times with parts of this chronology. Further detail is given below.

- 1867-1870 Half Moon Inn, 14 Bigg Market, Newcastle
- 1871-1872 Sycamore Street, Newcastle
- 1873-1878 Ridley Arms Public House, Pilgrim Street, Newcastle
- 1879-1893 Ridley Arms Yard Brewery, Pilgrim Street, Newcastle
- 1889-1956 Monkwearmouth Brewery, North Quay, Sunderland
- 1900-1956 Lochside Brewery, North East Road, Montrose, Tayside
- 1900-1929 1 George Street, Newcastle
- 1919-1922 Hedley Street Brewery, Newcastle

b) James Deuchar was born in Scotland in 1850 arriving in Newcastle upon Tyne in the 1860s along with his three older brothers Robert, George and Alexander (*NDBCC Newsletter* no.107 and Chilton & Poppleston. *The Early Brewing Trade on the Tyne*: unpublished mss. Newcastle Library c.1978)

c) His first directory listing is as a partner in Meikle & Deuchar at the Half Moon Inn from 1867-1870 with John Meikle and his brother George Deuchar.

James Deuchar from a newspaper obituary 17 December 1927

The *Dictionary of Business Biography* gives the Argyle public house, High Street, Gateshead as his first public house but he is not listed there in directories until 1887.

d) Acquiring the Ridley Arms and its brewery in the 1870s and the Monkwearmouth Brewery of J. J. & W. H. Allison c.1889 was the start of an empire of breweries, public houses and hotels.

e) James Deuchar Ltd was incorporated on 23 July 1894 as a brewer, maltster, wine, spirit and beer merchant, mineral and aerated water manufacturer, hotel, public house and beer-house proprietor and the restructured company was registered on 31 July 1898 with capital of £350,000 (*The Mineral Water Trade Recorder* October 1898).

f) In 1900 James Deuchar bought the Lochside Brewery of William Ross & Co. at Montrose to concentrate his brewing there, shipping the Montrose Lochside Ales to Newcastle's Quayside. In the same year he bought the successful mineral water manufacturing and bottling business of Robert Emmerson Junr at 1 George Street Newcastle continuing it under the former Montrose Brewery name of Ross & Co. The *Aerator & Bottler* June 1900 reported a public offer from James Deuchar Ltd of £150,000 of debenture stock of which £50,000 was "allotted to Mr. Robert Emmerson (Junr.) in part payment of the purchase money on properties already acquired by the company".

g) James Deuchar died on 12 December 1927 with an estate valued at £1,331,716. His business was eventually acquired by the Newcastle Breweries Ltd in 1956 (*Brewers & Bottlers of Newcastle upon Tyne*. Brian Bennison Newcastle 1995).

* * *

Dowson Brothers, Gateshead

(1) 10oz round-bottomed cylinder

The well-known firm of Dowson Brothers is the first of the four firms from Gateshead known to have used blue glass mineral water bottles. Their only confirmed type, a 10oz round-bottomed blue cylinder, is not common. The open embossing is on one side of the bottle as shown and consists of the firm's trade mark of a monogram of the letters **DB** inside a circle with **Dowson Brothers** above it and **Gateshead** below. The letter B in the monogram has internal divisions as will be seen in the letter G in the monograms on the Hamilton bottles of George Eland Newcastle (q.v.). There is the possibility of a blue bulb-neck codd from this firm (*NDBCC Newsletter* no. 25 June 1984) but no fragments are currently available to confirm its existence. The 10oz round-bottomed cylinder is illustrated.

Dowson Brothers 10oz round-bottomed cylinder

Notes:

a) In the twentieth century the firm advertised an establishment date of 1850 however the first trade directory record of the Dowson family in the mineral water trade is of Thomas Dowson in 1871. The title Dowson Brothers is not listed until 1883. The firm's advertisement shown is from Ward's Directory of Newcastle etc. 1889-90 and shows a splendid contemporary engraving of a mineral water manufactory interior which may (or may not) depict that of Dowson Brothers.

b) Trade directories list various Dowson family members as mineral water manufacturers and ale and porter merchants at the following addresses:

- 1871-1879 Oakwellgate, Gateshead
- 1879-1912 Victoria Street, Gateshead
- 1894-1908 Bush Inn, 28 Oakwellgate, Gateshead
- 1897-1904 British Queen Inn, 176 High Street, Gateshead
- 1913-1951 8 Kyle Place, Newcastle upon Tyne

c) The business is listed under the following titles at Oakwellgate:

- 1871-1874 Thomas Dowson
- 1875-1876 Robert Dowson
- 1876-1878 R. & H. Dowson
- 1879 Robert Dowson & brother

d) The proprietors of Dowson Brothers at Victoria Street are:

- 1883-1889 Henry and Robert Dowson
- 1884 Henry, Robert and Thomas Dowson
- 1889-1896 Joseph, Henry and Robert Dowson
- 1897-1908 Joseph, Henry, Robert and Thomas Dowson
- 1909-1912 Robert Dowson

The residence of R. Dowson is listed as Barn Close House Victoria Street in 1879.

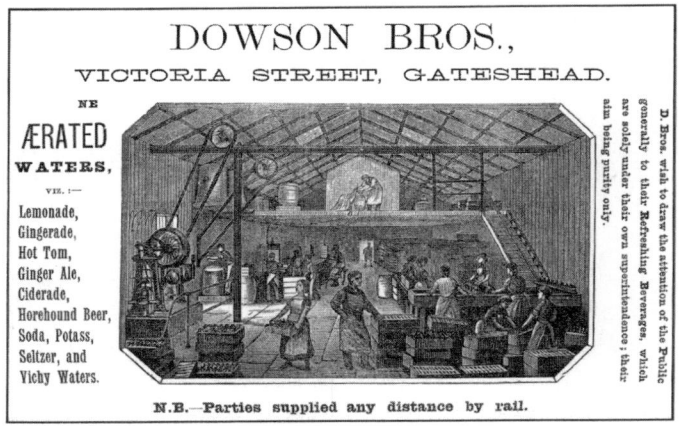

Advertisement from Ward's Directory of Newcastle 1889-90

e) The 1881 census records a Henry Dowson (aged 24), soda water manufacturer, employing two men, five boys and three women. Born in Hamsterley, County Durham he was living at Back Victoria Street in Gateshead with his wife Jane and three daughters.

f) The British Queen Inn and the Bush Inn are listed under the name of Robert Dowson. Thomas Dowson and a John Dowson are listed individually as mineral water manufacturers in 1895 but could well have been working for Dowson Brothers.

g) Robert and Henry Dowson trading as Dowson Brothers applied to register a monogram of the letters DB as a trade mark in Class 44 (no. 74,068) for mineral and aerated waters on 19 March 1888 claiming its use for 15 years before 1875.

> 74,068. Mineral and Aërated Waters, Natural and Artificial, including Ginger Beer. ROBERT DOWSON and HENRY DOWSON, trading as DOWSON BROTHERS, Victoria Street, Gateshead-on-Tyne, Mineral Water Manufacturers and Ale and Porter Merchants.—19th March 1888. Mark used by applicants and predecessors in business fifteen years before the 13th August 1875.

Trade mark registration of Dowson Brothers

h) Dowson Brothers was part of a local consortium who tried (unsuccessfully) to form the Northern Bottle Manufacturing Co. Ltd in 1892 (*NDBCC newsletter* no. 95).

i) *The Mineral Water Trade Journal* September 1911 reported a Deed of Arrangement:

Robert Dowson, trading as Dowson Bros., 1 Victoria Street, and residing at 162 Lodhouse Bank, Sheriff Hill, both Gateshead, mineral water manufacturer. Secured creditors, £90; liabilities, unsecured, £466; estimated net assets £201. Trustee: Mr. W. Blakey, 23 Pilgrim Street, Newcastle on Tyne

j) The firm's 1913 directory entry reads "Now removed to 8 Kyle Place Newcastle" where the business is listed adjacent to Wilkinson & Co., brewers, Newcastle who are noted in that year as "proprietors of Dowson Bros". Wilkinson & Co. continued to use the Dowson Brothers name until 1951 and was taken over by Hope & Anchor Breweries Ltd in 1954.

k) *The Mineral Water Trade Journal* September 1915 recorded the unexpected death at Sheriff Hill, Gateshead of Alderman Robert Dowson aged 66. It says that his association with the town council dated from 1899 and that he was elected an alderman in 1910.

Robert Dowson from Northern Gossip 3 January 1902

* * *

G. Eland, Newcastle

(1) 10oz Hamilton (GE's/PW/CS – N/ Established 1837)
(2) 10oz Hamilton (GE's/PW/CS/WR/N – Established 1837/ TM) (chisel-lip)
(3) 10oz Hamilton (GE's/PW/CS/WR/N – Established 1837/ TM)
(4) 6oz Hamilton (GE's/MW/CS/WR/N – Established 1837/ TM)
(5) 6oz Hamilton (GE/CS/N – Established 1837/TM)
(6) 6oz Hamilton (GE/CS/N – Established 1837/TM) (chisel-lip)
(7) 10oz Hamilton (GE's/SW/CS/WR/N – Established 1837/ TM) (chisel-lip)
(8) 10oz Hamilton (GE's/PW/N – TM)
(9) 10oz Hamilton (GE's/PW/CS/WR/N – TM)

To collectors, the blue Hamiltons of George Eland of Newcastle are probably the most familiar blue glass mineral water bottles from the North East. Although nine variations are detailed here there may well be more yet to be recorded. All bottles have conventional blob-tops for cork-stoppers apart from types (2) (6) and (7) which have chisel-lips. For ease of reference in the list above I have summarised the embossing on each side of each type in brackets (the sides separated by a hyphen) using the following abbreviations GE's

= G. Eland's, GE = G. Eland, PW = Potass Water, MW = Mineral Water, SW = Soda Water, CS = Cross Street, N = Newcastle, WR = Westgate Road, TM = Trade Mark,

Type (1) is a 10oz Hamilton embossed **G. Eland's/ Potass Water/ Cross Street** on one side and **Newcastle/ Established AD 1837** on the other. There is no trade mark embossed. Both sides are illustrated.

G. Eland 10oz Hamilton type (1)

G. Eland 10oz Hamilton type (1) reverse

Type (2) is a 10oz Hamilton, often seen with a long elegant chisel-lip, and is probably the most familiar type from the firm. It is embossed on one side in five lines **G. Eland's/ Potass Water/ Cross Street/ Westgate Road/ Newcastle** and on the other **Established AD 1837** along with the firm's trade mark of the letters **GE**. The letter G in the trade mark has distinctive internal divisions. Both sides are illustrated.

Type (3) is a 10oz Hamilton which is the same as type (2) but has a conventional blob-top instead of a chisel-lip (not illustrated).

Type (4) is a rare 6oz Hamilton with Mineral Water as its named contents. It is embossed on one side in five lines **G. Eland's/ Mineral Water/ Cross Street/ Westgate Road/ Newcastle** and on the other **Established AD 1837** along with the firm's trade mark. Both sides are illustrated.

G. Eland 10oz Hamilton type (2)

G. Eland 10oz Hamilton type (2) reverse

G. Eland 6oz Hamilton type (4)

G. Eland 6oz Hamilton type (4) reverse

Type (5) is another 6oz Hamilton of which a handful were dug in 1985 on an NDBCC dig at Blyth in Northumberland. The embossing reads **G. Eland/ Cross Street/ Newcastle** on one side and **Established AD 1837** on the other along with the firm's trade mark. The word Eland has no letter S on the end and the contents are not specified. Both sides are illustrated.

G. Eland 6oz Hamilton type (5)

G. Eland 6oz Hamilton type (5) reverse

Type (6) is a 6oz Hamilton which is the same as type (5) but has a lip which is neither a true chisel or a true blob-top. It does not appear to have been altered and I have classified it as a chisel-lip although it is possible that it is an isolated manufacturing fault (not illustrated).

Type (7) is the firm's rare 10oz Hamilton with Soda Water as the named contents. It has a chisel-lip and is embossed **G. Eland's/ Soda Water/ Cross Street/ Westgate Road/ Newcastle** on one side and **Established AD 1837** along with the firm's trade mark on the other. Both sides are illustrated.

G. Eland 10oz Hamilton type (7)

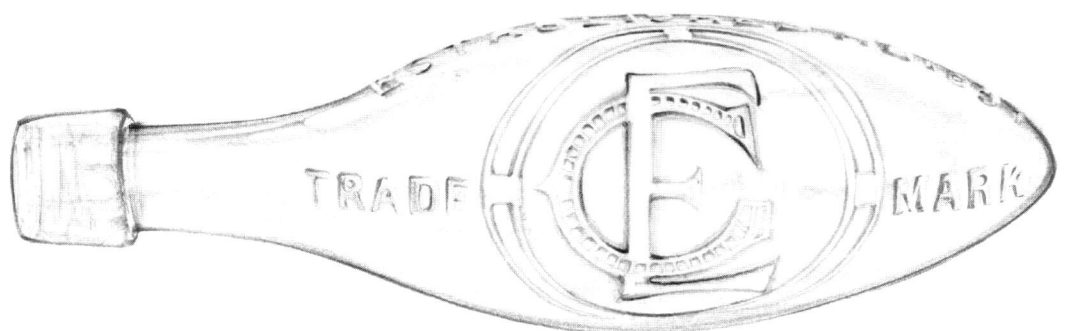

G. Eland 10oz Hamilton type (7) reverse

Type (8) is a rare 10oz Hamilton embossed **G. Eland's/ Potass Water/ Newcastle** on one side and on the other with the firm's trade mark without the Established AD 1837 details. The letter **G** in the trade mark is also noted to be plain and lacks the distinctive internal divisions seen in all the other examples from the firm. Both sides of type (8) are illustrated.

G. Eland 10oz Hamilton type (8)

G. Eland 10oz Hamilton type (8) reverse

Type (9) is a 10oz Hamilton with a conventional blob-top and is embossed **G. Eland's/ Potass Water/ Cross Street/ Westgate Road/ Newcastle** on one side in five lines using the same words seen on type (2). However the letters are significantly smaller and their layout shows that the bottle is from a different mould. The other side has the firm's trade mark but, like type (8), it lacks the Established AD 1837 wording. Both sides are illustrated.

G. Eland 10oz Hamilton type (9)

G. Eland 1oz Hamilton type (9) reverse

Notes:

a) George Eland is listed in Newcastle upon Tyne as follows:
- 1873-1878 G. Eland, mineral water manufacturer, 60 Westgate Road
- 1879-1910 G. Eland, mineral water manufacturer, 5 Cross Street

b) George Eland was born in London in 1840. He married Elizabeth Lodge in Newcastle in 1864 and is listed in the 1871 census as a mineral water manufacturer. He died in Newcastle in 1891 aged 51. His widow died in Newcastle in 1904 aged 67 (*NDBCC newsletter* no 119).

c) *The Mineral Water Trade Review and Guardian* December 1884 has a report from a traveller for the paper of a visit to Newcastle where he noted some "very large and showy placards, which depicted a snowstorm scene.... stuck upon all the hoardings" which bore the words "G. Eland's Hot Tom, a new winter beverage. No orders solicited, Newcastle" so he visited the firm reporting that:

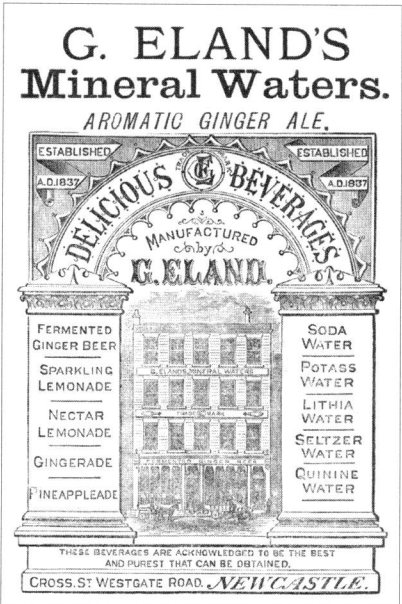

Advertisement from Health Resorts of Northumberland and Durham (Ellis 1894)

I made my way over to Mr. Eland's wonderfully neat, clean, smart, and well-fitted works in Cross Street, and introduced myself...Mr. E. at once greeted me heartily, asked me into his office, apologized for not being a subscriber to the *Review* and politely requested me to have his name put on our list at once, and to send him as a favour our last issue to commence with…Mr. Eland is a trifle independent, he employs no travellers, because he doesn't believe in cutting down prices, or doing a low-class trade, and he told me that he manufactured a labelled better grade goods, to order for some local chemists, and I saw he had a large number of their bin cases in his works.

d) The promotional article below is an advertising feature from *Tyneside Industries* (1889) although some of the factual details in it are not borne out by other research. The 1837 establishment date at Grainger Street is the date Eland used prominently on most of his blue glass mineral water bottles. His first directory listing, however, is in 1873 on Westgate Road and the Grainger Street business that the 1837 date refers to is not known. I have edited out the non-specific parts which give no details about the firm or its products.

George Eland, Mineral Water Manufacturer, Cross Street

One of the oldest and most renowned business establishments is that of Mr. G. Eland, the celebrated mineral water manufacturer at the address above. The business has been in existence over half a century having been established in 1837 in Grainger Street. Owing to the increasing demand for Mr. Eland's productions, the business was removed to more commodious premises in Westgate Road, and in 1876 it was found necessary, owing to the continued increase of business, to remove to the present premises, which were specially constructed for the trade... The premises cover an area of over four hundred square yards and have a frontage of upwards of forty-two yards. In the basement are the cellars etc. used for storing, where a large number of bottles, both filled and empty are kept...manufacture is carried on in the apartments on the ground floor, where the works are admirably equipped with all the latest machinery and appliances...The various processes are carried out under the immediate personal superintendence of the proprietor... On the floor above the ground floor flat are the stores and warehouses, where the majority of the manufactured commodities are kept, and here there is always a very large and varied stock of the most popular beverages. The next floor is used in preparing the water used in the various processes, and contains half a dozen large cisterns specially built for this purpose. On the uppermost floor is the "preparing room" ...set apart for making and storing the various syrups used in flavouring...over twenty hands are engaged... mineral waters manufactured, include all the most popular varieties, in addition to several that have been introduced...leading features of the business (are)..."Fermented Ginger Beer" (and)..."Aromatic Ginger Ale". The trade...embraces all parts of the north of England and many parts of Scotland.

e) An original advertising card from the firm (date unknown) gives the cost of Eland's potass water and soda water at "1/6d a dozen" each but does not specify the bottle size.

* * *

Emmerson Brothers, Newcastle

(1) 6oz cylinder
(2) 6oz Patent Safe Groove Codd

Two types of blue glass mineral water bottles are known from Emmerson Brothers of Newcastle. The 6oz cylinder has a conventional blob-top and is embossed on one side with the entwined initials **EB** with **Emmerson Bros** above it and **Newcastle** below. The base is plain. The bottle is shorter in height than other 6oz cylinders by up to ⅝" (16mm) yet holds exactly 6oz to the brim due to its slightly broader body.

The 6oz Emmerson Brothers Codd has never been a common bottle and there are still only a handful of complete examples known. No traces of a 10oz size are recorded. It is embossed with the firm's trade mark of the entwined letters **EB** with **Emmerson Bros** above it and **Newcastle** below. The back of the bottle is embossed **Patent Safe Groove/ Dan/ Rylands/ Barnsley**. There has been some confusion in the past about this firm and its trade mark and it is worth noting here that the penny-farthing trade mark was used exclusively by R. Emmerson Junr and does not appear on this, or any other, bottle from Emmerson Brothers. Both the cylinder and the Codd of Emmerson Brothers are illustrated.

Notes:
a) Despite extensive research the actual title Emmerson Brothers has not been found in any of the many documentary local history sources consulted.
b) The site of the partnership's manufactory is known from a stoneware stout bottle which is impressed Emmerson Brothers, Burton Brewery, Newcastle on Tyne. The Burton Brewery was the base of the family firm of R. Emmerson & Sons which was founded by Robert Emmerson (senior) in 1853 and became a major brewer & maltster, wine & spirit importer, ale & porter merchant, innkeeper and mineral water manufacturer in Newcastle. The Licensing Registers show that all of the firm's property appears solely under the R. Emmerson & Sons name from 1877 until the 1950s. Robert Emmerson (senior) is last listed as part of the business in 1883 and several of his sons are listed as partners in R. Emmerson & Sons:

Emmerson Brothers 6oz cylinder   Emmerson Brothers 6oz Codd

- 1877-1878 John, Robert Junr
- 1879-1882 John, Robert Junr, Henry
- 1883-1892 John, Henry, Edward
- 1893-1896 Henry, Edward
- 1898-1902 Edward
- 1903-1935 Henry

The oldest son, Robert Emmerson Junr, left the family firm to set up his own very successful bottling business c.1885 which is covered in the next company entry.

c) A promotional article on R. Emmerson & Sons in *A Descriptive Account of Newcastle: Illustrated* (c.1894) describes the mineral water manufactory at the Burton Brewery which can be identified in the engraving shown below which accompanied the article:

On the right of the entrance is a long two-storey building, used as a mineral water manufactory, and fitted with the most improved plant and machinery for generating the gas, bottling, corking and all the other various operations…Seltzer, lithia, potass, soda, lemonade, ginger beer, and similar beverages of the best quality are turned out in large quantities…many thousand bottles of mineral water can be turned out daily…a powerful steam engine supplies power to the mineral water factory.

d) A report in *The Mineral Water Trade Recorder* July 1895 refers to the aerated waters of "Messrs. R. Emmerson & Sons" but does not name Emmerson Brothers. No mineral water bottles embossed R. Emmerson & Sons have been recorded other than soda water syphons and it is a reasonable assumption that Emmerson Brothers was formed as a subsidiary company at the Burton Brewery on Sandyford Road (see also *NDBCC newsletter* 115 and Robertson 2012).

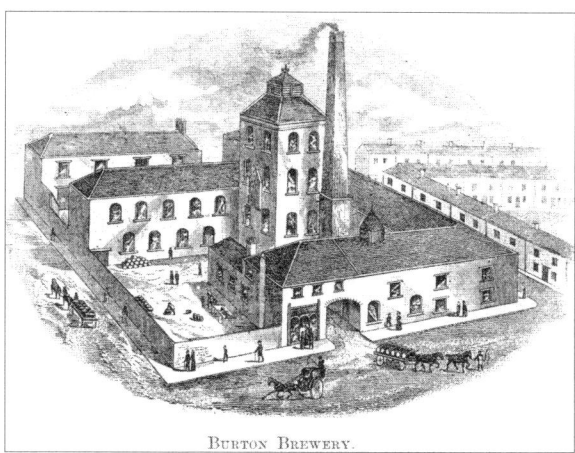

The Burton Brewery from *A Descriptive Account of Newcastle* c.1894

e) The title Ryland's Patent Safe Groove in the embossing refers to a tool used to make the groove inside the lip of the bottle. Dan Rylands patented his own groove-making tool in 1885 after a dispute with his former partner Hiram Codd which ended in court over a tool patented by Codd & Foster. Bottles made with Dan Rylands own patented tool were embossed "Ryland's Patent Safe Groove" from 1885 dating the Codd here to post-1885 (Mark Potten pers. com.).

f) In summary the Codd dates to post-1885 and the lack of the A10 mark suggests a pre-1891 date although precise dates for the firm are lacking.

* * *

R. Emmerson Junior, Newcastle

A famous name and a celebrated range of bottles all with the firm's well-known trade mark of a man riding a penny-farthing bicycle. Nine different types of blue glass bottles are currently known from R. Emmerson Junr. On eight of these the trade mark appears in one of two sizes which collectors refer to as the small and the large trade mark. The ninth type has an open trade mark. Below I have catalogued them according to the trade mark size and abbreviated significant differences in brackets after each type.

Small Trade Mark

(1) 6oz cylinder (A10 on the base)
(2) 6oz cylinder (plain base)
(3) 6oz cylinder (chisel-lip, plain base)
(4) 10oz cylinder (plain base)
(5) 10oz cylinder (chisel-lip, plain base)

Large Trade Mark

(6) 6oz cylinder (plain base)
(7) 10oz cylinder (A10 on the base)
(8) 10oz round-bottomed cylinder

Open Trade Mark

(9) 10oz Hamilton

All nine types have conventional blob-tops unless otherwise stated. The bases of the cylinders either have a broad central depression embossed with the A10 mark, a broad central depression which is plain or a small central "cut out" depression which is plain. None of them, unfortunately, has a maker's mark. The most recent two types of blue glass bottles from Robert Emmerson Junior have only appeared within the last five years and so the existence of further types is quite possible. The existence of a blue Codd from this firm has long been hoped for by collectors but no evidence of one is available at this time.

The Small Trade Mark

The small trade mark design encloses the names **R. Emmerson Junr** and **Newcastle**. In the centre of the design is the man on a penny-farthing bicycle trade mark below the words **Trade Mark**. The penny-farthing faces left on all five small trade mark types. As a general rule the embossing of the small trade mark tends to be much less bold than the large trade mark.

There are three types of 6oz cylinders with the small trade mark. Type (1) has a conventional blob-top, a smooth shoulder and a broad base embossed **A10**. Type (2) also has a conventional blob-top but with a plain small cut-out base (not illustrated). Type (3) is the same as type (2) but has a short straight-sided chisel-lip. Types (1) and (3) are illustrated.

R. Emmerson Junr 6oz cylinder type (1)   R. Emmerson Junr 6oz chisel-lip cylinder type (3)

The two types of 10oz cylinders with the small trade mark are both quite elegant bottles. Type (4) has a conventional blob-top, a smooth shoulder, a graceful neck and the base with a small plain central depression. Type (5) is the same as type (4) but has a long and elegant chisel-lip. Types (4) and (5) are illustrated.

R. Emmerson Junr 10oz cylinder type (4)   R. Emmerson Junr 10oz chisel-lip cylinder type (5)

The Large Trade Mark

The large trade mark design has many of the features seen in the small trade mark but there are significant differences. It is a significantly larger oval shape and encloses the name **R. Emmerson Junr** with the full name **Newcastle on Tyne** rather than just Newcastle as seen in the small trade mark. In the centre of the design we see the man on a penny-farthing bicycle trade mark again below the words **Trade Mark**. The penny-farthing is facing right on type (6) but reverts to facing left on types (7) and (8).

All three large trade mark types have conventional blob-tops. Type (6) is a 6oz cylinder with a broad plain base. Type (7) is a 10oz size with a broad base embossed with **A10**. Type (8) is a 10oz round-bottomed cylinder. Types (6), (7) and (8) are illustrated.

R. Emmerson Junr 6oz cylinder type (6)   R. Emmerson Junr 10oz cylinder type (7)   R. Emmerson Junr 10oz round-bottomed cylinder type (8)

Open Trade Mark

The final example, type (9), is a rare 10oz Hamilton with a conventional blob-top. It is embossed **R. Emmerson Junr** and **Newcastle on Tyne** on one side and on the other an open design of the man on a penny-farthing bicycle trade mark facing right above the words **Trade Mark**. Both sides of type (9) are illustrated.

Notes:

a) Robert Emmerson Junior is listed in Newcastle as a wholesale & family wine & spirit merchant, aerated water manufacturer, innkeeper and bottler of Bass and Allsopps ales and the Doctor's Genuine Dublin Stout. His main listing is as follows:

R. Emmerson Junr 10oz Hamilton type (9)

R. Emmerson Junr 10oz Hamilton type (9) reverse

- 1883-1901 R. Emmerson Junr, 1 George Street
- 1883-1901 R. Emmerson Junr, Farmer's Inn, 98 Scotswood Road
- 1897-1901 R. Emmerson Junr, 12 Elswick East Terrace

b) He was born in 1850, at Shotley, the eldest son of Robert Emmerson (senior) who founded the large brewing and bottling concern of R. Emmerson & Sons at the Burton Brewery in Newcastle upon Tyne (see Emmerson Brothers and *NDBCC newsletter* 115). From 1877-1883 he is listed as part of the parent firm R. Emmerson & Sons and appears under that firm at the Farmers Inn, 98 Scotswood Road and the Royal Oak, 222 Scotswood Road 1881-1883.

c) *Tyneside Industries* (1889) has a promotional article on Robert Emmerson Junior along with an engraving of his George Street manufactory as shown below. The following is an extract.

John Arkle 6oz Hamilton

Bewick Bros. 6oz Hamilton

F. Bradford 10oz flat-bottomed Hamilton Type (4)

Bradford Bros. 6oz flat-bottomed
Hamilton Type (1)

Bradford Bros. 10oz flat-bottomed
Hamilton Type (3)

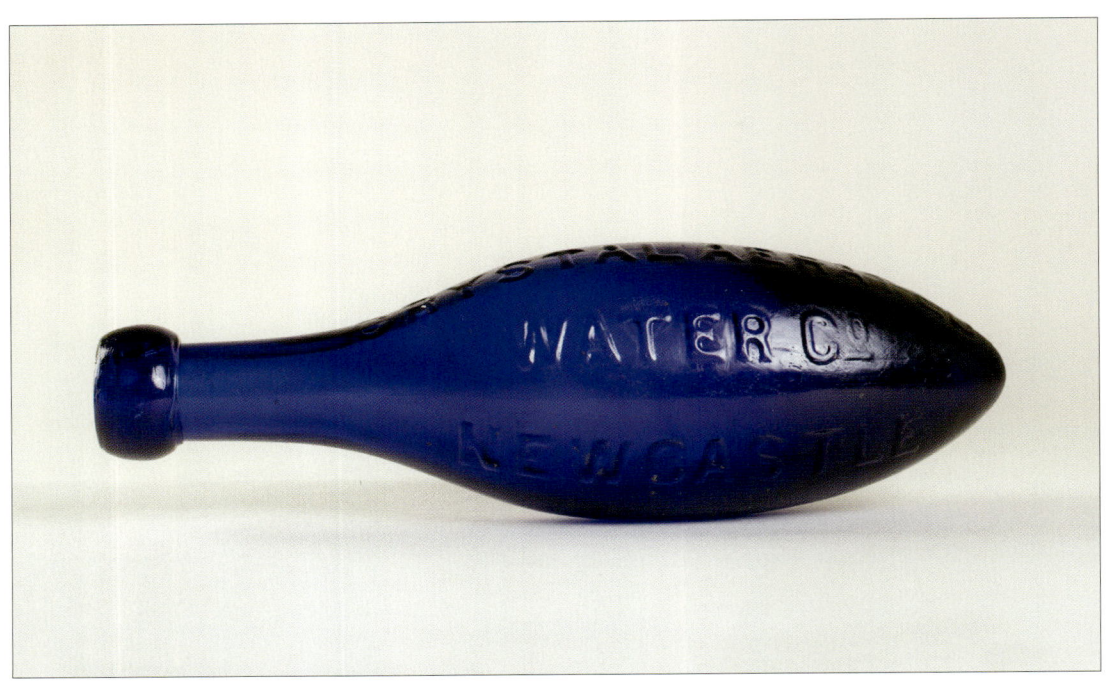

Crystal Aerated Water Co. 10oz Hamilton

Dowson Bros. 10oz round-bottomed cylinder

G. Eland 10oz Hamilton Type (2)

G. Eland 10oz Hamilton Type (2) – reverse

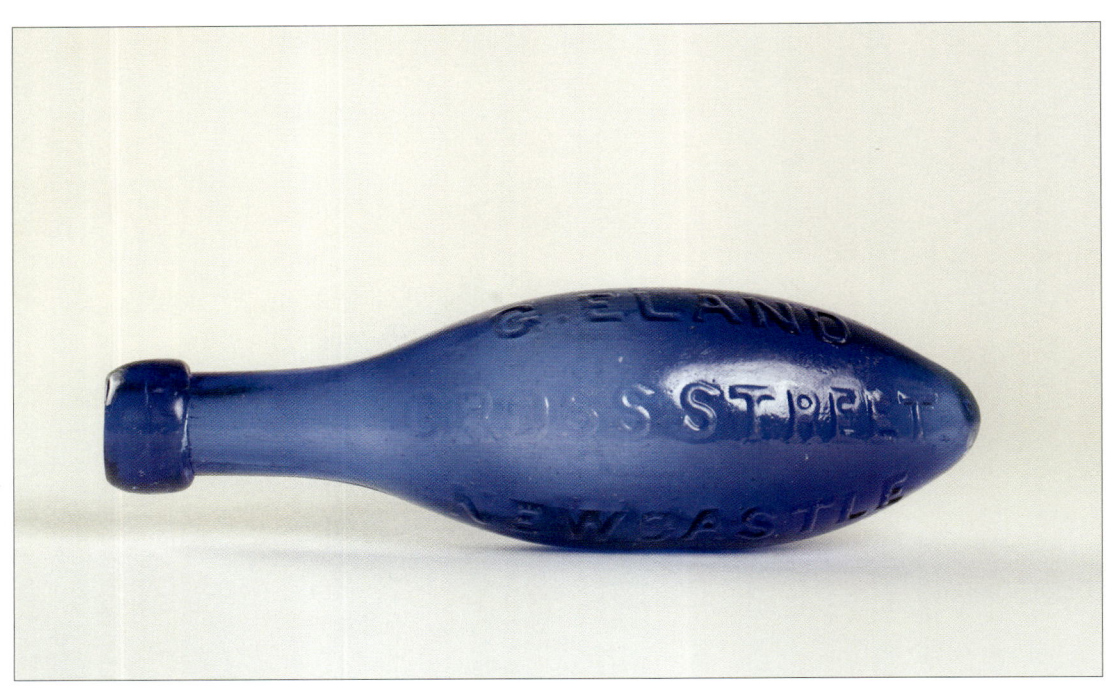

G. Eland 6oz Hamilton Type (5)

G. Eland 6oz Hamilton Type (5) – reverse

G. Eland 10oz Hamilton Type (7)

G. Eland 10oz Hamilton Type (8)

Emmerson Bros. 6oz Codd

Emmerson Bros. 6oz cylinder

R. Emmerson Jnr 6oz cylinder Type (1)   R. Emmerson Jnr 10oz cylinder Type (4)

R. Emmerson Jnr 6oz cylinder Type (6)

R. Emmerson Jnr 10oz round-bottomed cylinder Type (8)

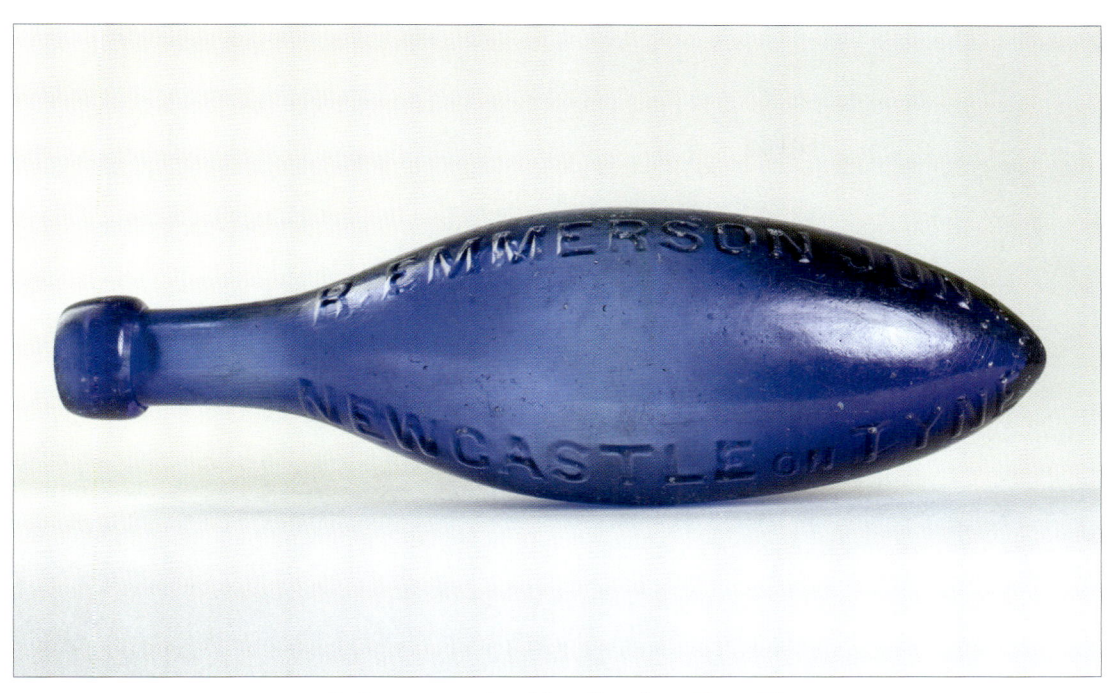

R. Emmerson Jnr 10oz Hamilton Type (9)

R. Emmerson Jnr 10oz Hamilton Type (9) – reverse

Fleet's 10oz cylinder

Fleet's 10oz cylinder – reverse

Walter Forbes 10oz cylinder

Gilpin 10oz Hamilton Type (5)

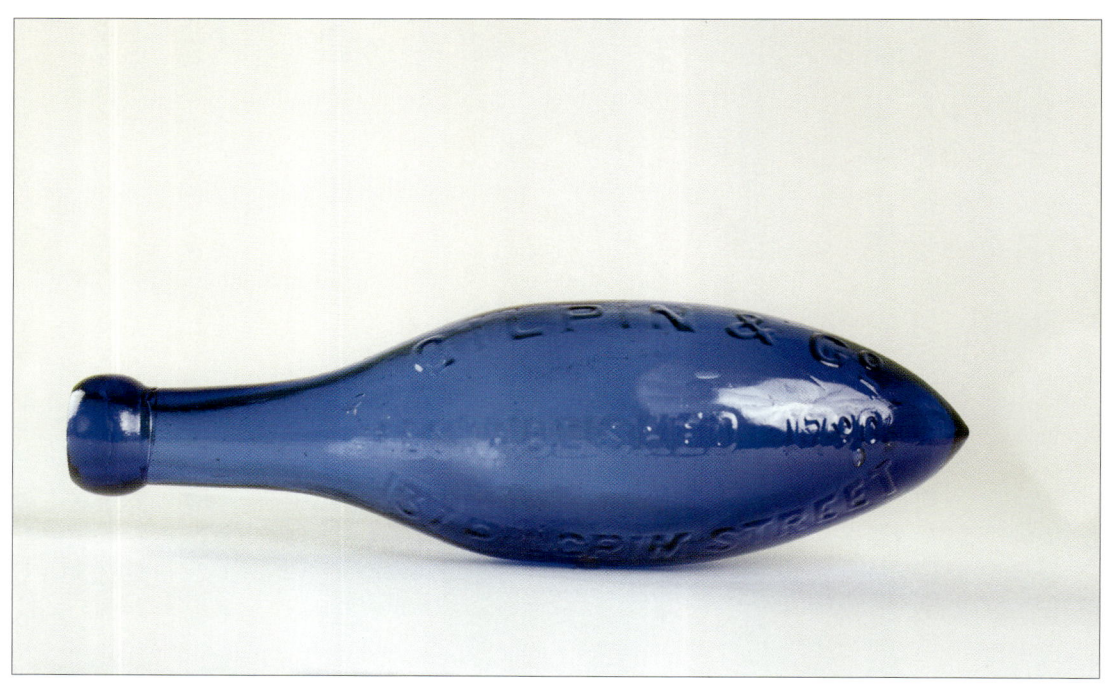
Gilpin 10oz Hamilton Type (2)

Gilpin 10oz Hamilton Type (3)

Gilpin 10oz Hamilton Type (3) – reverse

Glendenning 6oz round-bottomed cylinder

J. G. Graham 10oz Hamilton

R. Emmerson Jnr., Aerated Water Manufacturer, 1 George Street, Scotswood Road.

The business was established in 1882 in the present premises, which are very extensive and of commanding appearance, having a frontage of fully fifty yards... On the first floor of the building are a spacious suite of well-appointed offices and counting-house, the soda-water making department and the bottle-stand room. Above is a well-fitted laboratory...also extensive storerooms (and) joiners' shop...The cellarage accommodation is...adapted for the purpose of bottling and storage of beers, etc. At the back of the factory are excellent stables and yard, nine horses being kept. All the machinery and plant...amongst which may be mentioned double soda-water machines and pumps, the anti-atmospheric generator, turnover, corking racks, and nipple-bottling machines; the whole being from the works of Mr. Dan Rylands... The motive power is from a four horsepower Stockport gas engine. Mr. Emmerson is at present greatly extending his works, and fitting up new plant for the brewing of non-alcoholic hop ale. He is also fitting up a hoist...and connecting the four floors of the building...Upwards of thirty hands being regularly employed...The business in every department receives the personal attention of the proprietor...Mr. R. Emmerson has a business connection, extending to all parts of the town and district.

R. Emmerson Junior's manufactory from Tyneside Industries 1889

d) The Licensing Registers record a "Robert Emmerson the younger" as property owner and licence holder at 1 George Street who first applied to sell beer, wines and spirits there on 31 August 1886.

e) The Farmer's Inn at 98 Scotswood Road is listed as the main address for the firm along with George Street until 1894. R. Emmerson Junr is also listed as an innkeeper in the 1890s at the following public houses in Newcastle: the Cleveland Arms Bigg Market, the Empress Hotel Side, the William IV 209 Westgate Road, the Princess Restaurant 39 Groat Market, the Royal Court Grill Bigg Market, the Moulders Arms Inn Scotswood Road and at 27 High St Gosforth.

f) The trade press noted him to be a member of the Northumberland & Durham Mineral Water and Ale & Porter Bottle Trade Protection Society Ltd and its treasurer in 1895. He joined with other local mineral water manufacturers in 1892 in an (unsuccessful) attempt to form the Northern Bottle Manufacturing Co. Ltd.

g) *The Mineral Water Trade Review and Guardian* April 1885 reported the firm as advertising new aerated beverages called "Cham" and "Appleade" by means of "excruciatingly screaming burlesque comic show-cards". The same periodical in July 1885 reported that:

> Mr. Emmerson Jun., of Newcastle-on-Tyne appears to be quite alive to the requirements of the times, and I hope the cyclists of the district may find that his "Doctor's Stout" and favourite mineral waters may have the desirable effect upon them which he claims for these commodities.

h) Robert Emmerson Junior was very active in registering variations of his penny-farthing trade mark not only in the usual trade mark classes 43 and 44, for alcoholic beverages and aerated waters respectively, but also in class 50 for use on corks, boxes, stoppers and in class 3 for medical and pharmacy substances. Registered trademarks have been found in Class 43 (no. 73,842), (no. 79,261) and (no. 168,000); in Class 44 (no. 4,347), (no. 168,001), (no. 173,262) and (no. 182,777); in Class 3 (no. 167,999) and in Class 50 (no. 152,517). The trade mark most relevant to the design on his blue glass mineral water bottles was applied for by Robert Emmerson Junior, 1 George Street, Scotswood Road, Newcastle upon Tyne, Aerated Water Manufacturer on 23 November 1883 (no. 34,347) in Class 44 for mineral and aerated waters with no use claimed for it prior to 1875.

No. 34,347 (see page 349).

Trade mark (no. 34,347) registration of Robert Emmerson Junior

i) Robert Emmerson Junior's business was acquired by James Deuchar Ltd of 18 Clayton Street Newcastle upon Tyne (q.v.) in 1900. In the same year James Deuchar acquired the Lochside Brewery in Montrose from William Ross & Co. and transferred the Ross & Co. name to R. Emmerson Junior's George Street business. He also became subsequent proprietor of his well-known Doctor's Stout trade mark no. 73,842 in November 1901. The *Aerator and Bottler* June 1900 reported the details of a James Deuchar Ltd public subscription offer of £150,000 of debenture stock "of which £50,000 was allotted to Mr. Robert Emmerson (Jnr.) in part payment of the purchase money on properties already acquired by the company".

* * *

Fleet, Birtley

(1) 10oz cylinder

Alexander Fleet was a notable bottler in the small township of Birtley and among his decoratively embossed range of bottles is a heavily made 10oz blue glass cylinder with a thick but otherwise conventional blob-top. Two deep blue examples of this bottle first appeared in 1987 and it has remained rare. Although it lacks the elegance of many of the Tyneside blue cylinders Fleet's example is still a nice addition to the North East blue glass catalogue. It is extensively embossed on both sides of the bottle. One side has four lines of writing detailing **Fleet's/ Aerated Waters/ Established AD 1869/ Birtley**. The other side has his pictorial registered trade mark consisting of the word **Registered** above the words **Nil Desperandum** arched over an arm holding a spear with the words **Trade Mark** and the registered numbers **8381 & 8382** below. It has no maker's mark and the base of the bottle has a broad central depression which is plain.

Notes:

a) Alexander Ramsay Fleet is listed as a grocer, ale, porter, wine & spirit merchant and mineral water manufacturer in Birtley, County Durham. Trade directory, trade press and census returns give the following chronology of A. R. Fleet's business in Birtley:
- 1869 founding date used by the firm
- 1873 grocer, ale & porter merchant
- 1875 aerated water manufacturer
- 1881 grocer, ale & spirit merchant, Brook Square (aged 40)
- 1891 grocer & mineral water manufacturer, 2 Fleet Square

Fleet's 10oz cylinder   Fleet's 10oz cylinder reverse

- 1894 grocer, ale & porter, wine & spirit merchant, mineral water manufacturer
- 1901 income tax collector, Coney House

The Licensing Registers show that A. R. Fleet held a wine, beer and spirits licence at 37 Orchard Street, Birtley from 26 August 1885 to 9 January 1895.

b)   Fleet claimed an establishment date of 1869 on many of his bottles which is consistent with his claim for prior use of his trade mark in his application for its registration (see below).

c)   Aerated water manufacture by Fleet is first noted in a testimonial dated 12 July 1875 for Codd's patent bottles in *The Mineral Water Trade Recorder* January 1876.

d) On 25 July 1876 Alexander Fleet applied to register his trade mark of an arm holding a spear under the words Nil Desperandum in Class 43 for fermented liquors and spirits and Class 44 for mineral and aerated waters. Both of these registrations were misprinted in the *Trade Mark Journal* announcement where they were given the same registration number 8382 (the numbers in the embossing will be seen to be 8381 and 8382). He claimed use of this trade mark for six years prior to 24 July 1876.

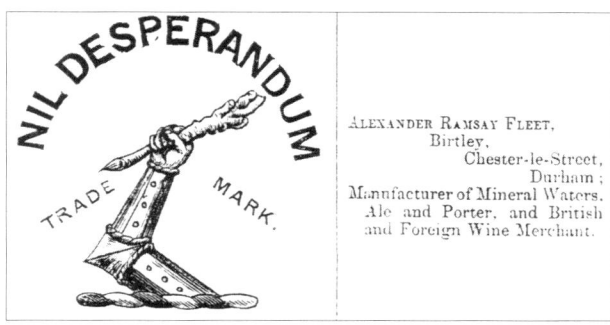

Trade mark registration of A. R. Fleet

* * *

Walter Forbes & Co., Edinburgh & Newcastle

(1) 10oz cylinder

The Edinburgh chemist and aerated water manufacturer Walter Forbes opened a branch mineral water manufactory in Newcastle upon Tyne c.1894. He continued to use his trade mark of a beaver on his glass and stoneware Newcastle bottles all of which are desirable to the collector.

The 10oz dark blue glass cylinder shown was unrecorded until an example appeared in 1993 which was said to have been dug in the Edinburgh area in that year. Very sick when found it has since been somewhat over-polished. It has a conventional blob-top for a cork-stopper and is embossed lengthways on one side of the bottle with the firm's title **Walter Forbes & Co.** above the trade mark of a beaver carrying a stick and the words **Trade Mark** with the two city names of **Edinburgh/ & Newcastle** in two lines below. It has no maker's mark and the base has a broad central depression which is plain.

Notes:
a) Walter Forbes & Co. is listed in Newcastle upon Tyne:
- 1894-1897 aerated water manufacturer, 100 Percy Street

b) The manufactory on Percy Street was taken over from the Nectar Cream Beverage Co. Ltd who in turn acquired it from John Mackay & Co. *The Mineral Water Trade Recorder* April 1892 records the address of the Nectar Cream Beverage Co. Ltd as being at the "Stag-yard, Percy-street, Newcastle upon Tyne". A brewery is listed at this site for the previous half century. The site's full bottling trades history listing is thus:

- 1834-1884 Percy Street Brewery (The Stag Brewery)
- 1885-1892 John Mackay & Co.
- 1892-1893 Nectar Cream Beverage Co. Ltd
- 1894-1897 Walter Forbes & Co.

c) Walter Forbes's business was based in Edinburgh where he traded from Beaverhall Bank as a chemist and mineral water manufacturer. The location being the obvious source for the firm's registered trade mark (see below). The Newcastle branch is listed only for the production of mineral waters.

d) *The Mineral Water Recorder* 1 January 1894 noted that the estates of Walter Forbes had been sequestered on 15 November 1893:

Walter Forbes, Edinburgh & Newcastle, chemist and aerated water manufacturer, late residing at 24, Beaverhall-terrace, Edinburgh, but now believed to be in Chicago, U.S.A. or elsewhere furth of Scotland. 15th November 1893. Election of Trustee and Commissioners: Dowdell's rooms, 18 George Street, Edinburgh, 27th November 1893. Claims by 15th March, 1894. Agents: Welsh and Forbes, 29 St Andrew-Square, Edinburgh S.S.C.

e) The Newcastle branch of Walter Forbes & Co. lasted only a few short years but despite the disappearance of Walter Forbes himself in 1893, as detailed above, the Beaverhall Bank Edinburgh business is mentioned in the mineral water trade press into the twentieth century.

f) Registration of the well-known trade mark of a beaver carrying a stick was applied for by Walter Forbes and James Hinde on 28 January 1890 in Class 44 (no. 95,419) for aerated and mineral waters.

Walter Forbes
10oz cylinder

Trade mark registration of Walter Forbes & Company

* * *

Gilpin & Co., Newcastle

James Gilpin was one of the earliest chemists in Newcastle upon Tyne to branch out into the manufacture of mineral waters and his business has an interesting history. Gilpin & Co. are known to have used a selection of blue glass mineral water bottles consisting of six types of 10oz Hamilton and one flat-bottomed 10oz Hamilton. In the list below for ease of reference I have summarised, in brackets, the embossing on each side of each type (the sides separated by a hyphen). Full details of the embossing on each type follows.

(1) 10oz Hamilton (Gilpin & Co/ 101 Pilgrim Street/ Newcastle on Tyne – plain)

(2) 10oz Hamilton (Gilpin & Co/ Established 1790/ 137 Pilgrim Street – Newcastle on Tyne)

(3) 10oz Hamilton (Gilpin/ Newcastle – Potass / Water) (chisel-lip)

(4) 10oz Hamilton (Gilpin/ Newcastle – Potass / Water)

(5) 10oz Hamilton (Gilpin & Co/ 137 Pilgrim St/ Newcastle on Tyne – Established 1790)

(6) 10oz flat-bottomed Hamilton (Gilpin & Co. – Established 1790)

(7) 10oz Hamilton (etched)

All the above types have a nominal 10oz capacity which generally measures up to 11oz brimful (i.e. including the corkage) as detailed in chapter one. The distinctive type (3) holds a generous 13½oz to the brim. All have conventional blob-tops apart from type (3) which has a short chisel-lip. Types (3) and (4) differ only in the shape of their lips. The latter has a more conventional blob-top and they may represent simple manufacturing variations rather than a deliberate change of style.

Type (1) is embossed **Gilpin & Co/ 101 Pilgrim St/ Newcastle on Tyne** on one side with the other side being plain. As detailed in the notes below this was the address of the ale & porter merchant side of Gilpin & Co.'s business from 1855-84 which was acquired by Bartleman & Crighton in 1869 along with the firm's soda water manufactory formerly run from the chemist's side of the business at 99 Pilgrim Street. This should date this bottle to 1869-84.

Gilpin & Co. 10oz Hamilton type (1)

Type (2) is embossed **Gilpin & Co/ Established 1790/ 137 Pilgrim Street** on one side and **Newcastle on Tyne** on the other. As detailed in the notes below this was the address of Gilpin & Co.'s ale & porter business from 1885-1904. This dates the bottle to this period when the firm was owned by Richard Thomas Wilson (1885-94) and John Rowell & Son Ltd (1894-1929). Both sides of type (2) are illustrated.

Gilpin & Co. 10oz Hamilton type (2)

Gilpin & Co. 10oz Hamilton type (2) reverse

Type (3) is a short-necked 10oz hamilton with a short chisel-lip and heavily embossed letters and, as already noted, holds a generous 13½oz brimful. One side is embossed **Gilpin** and **Newcastle** and the other side **Potass** and **Water** as shown with no specific address. This may be the earliest known type from the firm when the manufactory was part of the chemist & druggist business (pre-1869). Unusually the embossing reads from the pointed base back towards the lip of the bottle, a feature not seen on any other Hamilton in this book. Both sides of type (3) are illustrated.

Gilpin & Co. 10oz Hamilton type (3)

Gilpin & Co. 10oz Hamilton type (3) reverse

Type (4) is the same basic bottle as type (3) but has a conventional blob-top (not illustrated).

Type (5) has the same wording as type (2) but the letters are significantly larger and the layout is completely different. It is embossed **Gilpin & Co/ 137 Pilgrim St/ Newcastle on Tyne** on one side and **Established 1790** on the other. As for type (2) this should date to 1885-1904. Both sides of type (5) are illustrated

Gilpin & Co 10oz Hamilton type (5)

Gilpin & Co 10oz Hamilton type (5) reverse

Type (6) is a 10oz flat-bottomed Hamilton an example of which was first seen in 1997. It's embossed **Gilpin & Co.** on one side in large letters ⅞" (22mm) high and **Establd 1790** on the other in letters ¾" (19mm) high with the date in a different typeface. The broad base, 1⅞" (47mm) across, is embossed centrally with the letter **A** over **867**. In style it looks a later production than the Hamiltons. Both sides of type (6) are illustrated.

Type (7) is an unusual example that appeared at an NDBCC meeting in 2002. It has a circular etched design on one side only as shown consisting of a broken double circle containing the words **Gilpin & Compy Newcastle on Tyne** with the firm's trade mark of three castles in the centre with the words **Trade Mark** unusually orientated to be read with the bottle upright. The same etched design is known on other bottles from the firm.

As a firm whose origins date from the late eighteenth century Gilpin & Co. has a long and interesting history. There were two distinct parts to the business which operated from adjacent premises on Pilgrim Street. One was a chemist & druggist and the other an ale and porter merchant and cork-cutting business. The aerated water manufactory was initially under the chemist's side of the business but, as will be seen, moved to the ale

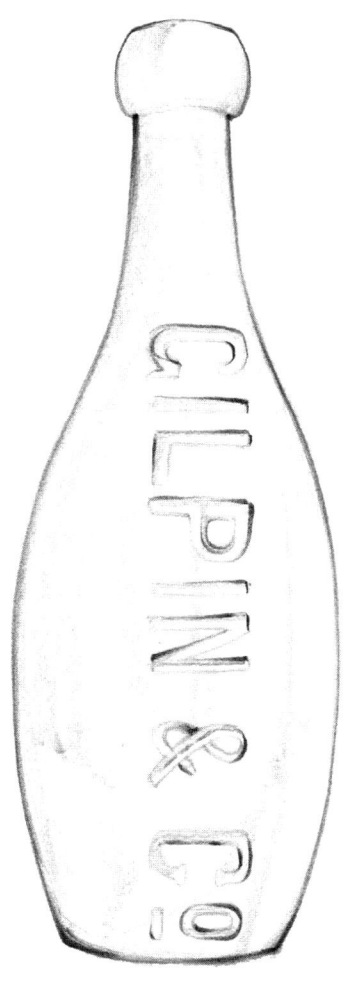

Gilpin & Co. 10oz flat-bottomed
Hamilton type (6)

Gilpin & Co. 10oz flat-bottomed
Hamilton type (6) reverse

Gilpin & Co. 10oz etched
Hamilton type (7)

& porter side c.1869. Sadly all the buildings disappeared in the 1960s redevelopment of Newcastle city centre which removed the lower part of Pilgrim Street. Even more sadly I was a student living in Newcastle at the time and could have looked over the site but bottle collecting was not then on my horizon. For ease of reference the two sides of the business are dealt with separately.

CHEMIST & DRUGGIST

a) This side of the business is listed in Newcastle as follows:
- 1801-1814 Pilgrim Street
- 1821-1854 53 Pilgrim Street
- 1855-1884 99 Pilgrim Street
- 1885-1903 135 Pilgrim Street

In the early years of the nineteenth century Pilgrim Street was unnumbered with locations sometimes simply been given as upper, lower or middle of the street. Numbering first appears in Pigot's national directory of 1820-21 & 1822. All the addresses above are the same location, the different numbers being due to renumbering of Pilgrim Street in the nineteenth century. The dates of the chemist's side of the business will be seen to parallel those of the next door ale, porter and cork part of the business detailed below.

b) The Pilgrim Street premises were of historic importance being fronted by "a fine old front house…an aldermanic residence in the eighteenth century" also used at one time as the "mansion occupied by H.M. Judges of Assize during their periodical visits to the town on circuit business" (traditionally they were housed at the Mansion House). It comprised a range of three-storey buildings with a frontage of 180 feet extending down Gilpin's Yard some 50 yards in length back to a delivery exit at Manors. The two parts of the business were in the same building "with the very high-class chemists' and druggists' in the front portion of the premises". Two carved stones from the towers of the Old Tyne Bridge (destroyed by the flood of 1771) were, after a short sojourn in a city Alderman's garden wall, set above the office doors of Gilpin & Co. One bore the city coat of arms dated 1646 and the other the arms of Bishop Crewe (*Tyneside Industries* 1890 and *A Descriptive Account of Newcastle Illustrated* c.1894).

c) The titles of the chemist & druggist side of the business below (with known proprietors in brackets) are from trade directories, the *Newcastle Chronicle* 26 April 1800, 1 February 1812 and 7 August 1813; Margaret Ellison (1975); *Schweppes the First 200 Years* (Douglas Simmons 1983) and *Bookplates by Beilby & Bewick* (Nigel Tattersfield 1999).

- 1800-1811 Anthony Clapham Junior (soda water manufacturer from 1812)
- 1812-1829 Clapham & Gilpin (Anthony Clapham and James Gilpin)
- 1833-1847 James Gilpin (James Gilpin)
- 1848-1858 Gilpin & Son (James & Benjamin Gilpin)
- 1859-1870 Gilpin & Co. (James Gilpin until 1868)
- 1871-1874 Gilpin & Beadel (Alfred Beadel)
- 1875-1880 Gilpin & Co.
- 1881-1886 Gilpin & Co; Mawson & Swan
- 1887-1895 Gilpin & Co; Mawson, Swan & Weddell
- 1896-1903 Mawson, Swan & Weddell

d) The chemist's business was founded by Anthony Clapham Junior in Pilgrim Street in 1800 when he advertised in the *Newcastle Chronicle* of 26 April 1800 as follows:

CHEMIST & DRUGGIST
ANTHONY CLAPHAM Jun

RESPECTFULLY informs his Friends and the Public in general that he has opened a shop in Pilgrim Street, opposite the Manor-Chare, Newcastle, where they may confide on being served with the best genuine Drugs and Chemicals on the most reasonable Terms; and by a steady Attention to Business he hopes to merit a share of their favours. N.B. Physicians Prescriptions and Family Recipes carefully made up. Patent Medicines sold genuine.

Trade directories list him there 1801-1811. In the *Newcastle Chronicle* on 1 February 1812 it was announced that James Gilpin had become his partner as follows:

A. CLAPHAM
Chemist & Druggist

RESPECTFULLY informs his Friends and the Public of Newcastle, and its Vicinity, that he has taken into Partnership his late Assistant, JAMES GILPIN, and the Business will in future be carried on under the Firm of CLAPHAM & GILPIN

Soda water manufacture by the firm is first mentioned in the account books of the famous engravers Beilby & Bewick (Ralph Beilby, brother of the Newcastle glass enameller William Beilby, and Thomas Bewick the celebrated wood engraver) which record an order on 13 June 1812 for a bottle mould to be engraved for "Clapham & Co. Mineral Water Newcastle" (Ellison 1975). Manufacture of soda water could have begun here earlier as a letter exists, dated 1808, sent by Anthony Clapham Junior of Newcastle to a Luke Howard of Essex (an analyst) about a soda water sample that the latter had sent him for his opinion (Simmons 1983). In 1813 the firm, using the title A. Clapham & Co., advertised its soda water business at Pilgrim Street in the *Newcastle Chronicle* 7 August 1813 stating it was already in operation at that time. Below is an extract from this.

SODA WATER

A. CLAPHAM & Co. Manufacturers of the above, beg Leave to inform their friends and the Public, that from a late Addition to their Apparatus for preparing Soda Water, they now have it in their Power to supply such Orders as they may be favoured with, without Delay; which the great Demand they have had for that Article, has hitherto occasionally prevented.
Pilgrim-street, Newcastle upon Tyne, 7th Month 30th, 1813

e) Whilst Anthony Clapham Junior founded the chemist and soda water business subsequently taken over by James Gilpin, his family had several other business interests in Newcastle in the late eighteenth and early nineteenth centuries as below. The advertised founding date of Gilpin & Co. of 1790 could be related to his former partner's brewery of that year (see also note (j) Brumell & Gilpin).

- 1778-1782 Clapham & King, brewers, Javelgroupe, Close, Newcastle
- 1790-1801 Anthony Clapham & Co., brewery, Javelgroupe
- 1795 Clapham & Partners, brewers, Javelgroupe
- 1805 Anthony Clapham, brewer, Pilgrim Street
- 1811 Clapham & Forster, soap manufacturers, Ouseburn
- 1822-1834 Anthony Clapham & Co., soap manuf., 52 Pilgrim Street & Ouseburn
- 1838 Anthony Clapham, alkali manuf., 43 Sandhill and Friar's Goose

f) James Gilpin is last listed at the business in 1868. After this date the listings show that the chemists and the ale & porter merchant sides of the business were under different owners although both sides confusingly still used the Gilpin name.

g) In 1869 the chemist's soda water manufactory was sold to the new owners of the ale & porter merchant side of the business as detailed below (see Bartleman & Crighton). The chemist & druggist business then continued under various new owners detailed in note (c). Between 1881-1895 the well-known name of Mawson & Swan, chemists, is listed alongside the Gilpin & Co. name until 1896 when the Gilpin name is finally dropped. From 1903 no chemist's business is listed at 135 Pilgrim Street.

ALE & PORTER MERCHANT and CORK MANUFACTURER

h) The listings of this side of the business at Newcastle parallel those of the chemist's side:

- 1814 Pilgrim Street
- 1821-1855 52 Pilgrim Street
- 1844-1904 5-7 Manors
- 1855-1884 101 Pilgrim Street
- 1885-1904 137 Pilgrim Street
- 1907-1929 72 Northumberland Street

The three addresses on Pilgrim Street are from a renumbering of Pilgrim Street as for the chemist & druggist side of the business and do not indicate a change of location. The Manors address is listed as a store. It was behind their premises and they have already been noted in note (b) to have had a delivery exit there.

i) The listed titles of this part of the business (with known proprietors' names in brackets) are:

- 1814-1834 Brumell & Gilpin (George Attley Brumell and James Gilpin)
- 1838-1841 Gilpin & Brumell (James Gilpin and George Attley Brumell)
- 1844-1868 Gilpin & Co. (James Gilpin)
- 1869-1874 Gilpin & Co. (Bartleman & Crighton)
- 1874-1884 Gilpin & Co. (George Richard Turnbull and Richard Thomas Wilson)
- 1885-1894 Gilpin & Co. (Richard Thomas Wilson)
- 1894-1929 Gilpin & Co. (John Rowell & Son Ltd)

j) **Brumell & Gilpin (1814-34)**

Brumell & Gilpin were "members of a respected Quaker family" (*Newcastle Illustrated* 1894). Prior to his 1814 partnership with James Gilpin, George Brumell is listed as a cabinet maker on Pilgrim Street:

- 1778-1782 George Brumell (also in 1801)
- 1790-1795 Brumell & Dunn

Gilpin & Co.'s advertised establishment date of 1790 could originate from this connection with George Brumell (see also under Anthony Clapham & Co. above).

The opening of Brumell & Gilpin's London Porter business in 1814 was announced in the *Newcastle Chronicle* and *Newcastle Courant* newspapers on 5 March 1814

BRUMELL AND GILPIN LONDON PORTER MERCHANTS

Respectfully inform their Friends and the Public of Newcastle and its Vicinity they have commenced the above Business, nearly opposite the George Inn, Pilgrim-Street and having formed a Connexion with Barclay, Perkins, and Co. they hope to be able to supply to their Friends, at all times, with an article of the best Quality; and by a punctual Attention to the Orders they may be favoured with, to merit a Share of public Support. Newcastle, 3d Month, 5th, 1814

Advertisement from Richardson's Directory of Newcastle 1838

In 1838 George Brumell is also listed as an insurance agent at 52 Pilgrim Street at which time the name of James Gilpin heads the partnership.

k) **Gilpin & Co. (1844-68)**

The ale & porter merchant side of the business is listed under this familiar title with James Gilpin as proprietor from 1844-1868. He is unlisted after 1868 after which the ale & porter business, like the chemists side of the business, found a new owner.

l) **Bartlemen & Crighton: Gilpin & Co. (1869-74)**

This North Shields brewer, which already had on outlet at 10 Grey Street in Newcastle, is listed as the owner of the ale, porter and cork manufacturing side of Gilpin & Co. from 1869-1874 importantly along with the aerated water manufactory formerly a part of the chemist & druggists side of the business. Their 1869 advertisement shown suggests they were rebranding the business under their name but no Bartleman & Crighton Newcastle bottles are known and their subsequent advertisements all use the Gilpin & Co. title.

Advertisement from Ward's Directory of Newcastle 1869-70

m) **Turnbull & Wilson (1874-84), Richard Wilson (1885-94)**

George Richard Turnbull and Richard Thomas Wilson are listed as proprietors of the ale & porter merchants, cork-cutting and aerated water manufacturers from 1874-1884. Richard Wilson is listed as the sole proprietor 1885-1894. Both continued to use the Gilpin & Co. name as in the advertisement of 1881 shown.

Advertisement from Wards Directory of Newcastle 1881

n) Gilpin & Company applied to register as a trade mark a circular device with the name of the firm and the city around the three castles part of the city's coat of arms on 9 August 1886 in Class 44 (no. 55,825) for mineral and aerated waters claiming a prior use of the mark from 1825.

Trade mark registration of Gilpin & Company

This mark has a historical relevance to the firm's premises from the Old Tyne Bridge stones sited above their main doorway as detailed in note (b).

o) Promotional articles on the firm in *Tyneside Industries* (1889) and *A Descriptive Account of Newcastle* (1894) note that the firm made gingerade, lemonade, soda water, and stocked Brighton seltzer water and bottled ales and stout from a wide selection of Burton and London brewers.

p) **John Rowell & Son Ltd (1894-1929)**

The ale & porter, cork-cutting and aerated water business of Gilpin & Co. was incorporated into the Gateshead brewers John Rowell & Son Ltd when that firm was registered on 29 March 1894 with £175,000 capital to acquire John Rowell & Son (brewers of Gateshead); J. M. Bruce (Newcastle); William Turnbull & Co. (brewers of South Shields) and Gilpin & Co. They continued to use the Gilpin name at Newcastle (moving to Northumberland

Street in 1907) and also at two other of their outlets at East Street Gateshead (listed 1903-1939) and 10 Front Street Consett (listed 1914-1929). John Rowell & Son Ltd was itself taken over by The Newcastle Breweries Ltd in 1959 and liquidated on 2 September 1960 (Richmond and Turton 1990).

* * *

Glendenning, Newcastle

(1) 6oz round-bottomed cylinder
(2) 10oz Hamilton

The Glendenning business in Newcastle was a wine merchant's that survived well into the twentieth century. It diversified into mineral water manufacture in the late nineteenth century and used at least two types of blue glass mineral water bottle. These are a 6oz round-bottomed cylinder and a 10oz Hamilton, examples of the latter first being recorded in the year 2000. Both bottles are embossed on one side only with the same attractive design of the firm's trade mark of a sword cleaving corn along with the words **Trade Mark** with **Glendenning** above it and **Newcastle** below. The bottles should date to 1873-1902 as outlined in note (d) below. Both types of bottle are illustrated.

Glendenning 6oz round-bottomed cylinder

Glendenning 10oz Hamilton

Notes:

a) The firm is listed as a wine & spirit merchant, importer and bonder under the titles:
- 1869-1893 William Glendenning
- 1894-1898 William Glendenning & Sons
- 1899-1953 William Glendenning & Sons Ltd

b) The firm is listed at the following addresses in Newcastle upon Tyne:
- 1869-1872 12 Clayton Street West
- 1873-1904 9 Grainger Street
- 1890-1938 33 St Mary's Place
- 1903-1918 26 Blackett Street
- 1919-1953 Hood Street
- 1936-1953 131 Elswick Road

c) *The Mineral Water Trade Recorder* of June 1899 reported the registration of the limited company of W. Glendenning & Sons Ltd as follows:

A limited liability company has been formed to take over the business of Messrs. W. Glendenning & Sons, Newcastle upon Tyne, as wine and spirit merchants and manufacturers of aerated waters. Capital £30,000 in £5 shares. Messrs. W. Glendenning, W. G. Glendenning and G. H. Glendenning are the first directors.

d) Mineral water manufacture is listed from 1887 to 1902 with the manufactory at 33 St Mary's Place. According to Terry Glendenning, great-grandson of the firm's founder, this was the former premises of the Geographical Institute which the firm equipped with the latest bottling and machinery with offices and blending rooms on the first floor (*NDBCC Newsletter* no. 96). The firm was, however, making mineral waters before 1887. A known silkscreen advertisement from W. Glendenning at 9 Grainger Street (private collection) contains an endorsement of their mineral waters from *The Lancet* dated 1884. The same name and address also appears on another poorly preserved advertisement for the firm's mineral waters (part shown below) which should date to 1873-1893.

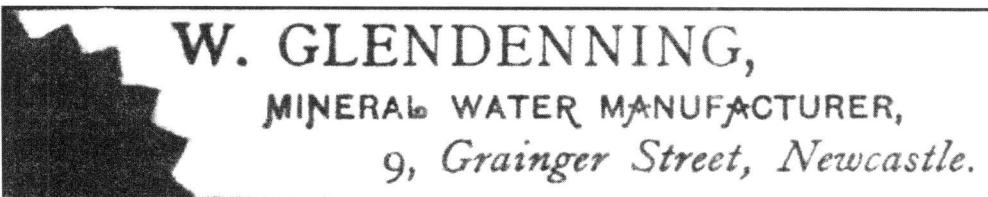

W. Glendenning advertisement c.1873-93

e) The founder of the firm, William Glendenning, was born in Sunderland. In 1851 his trade was a blacksmith and he was living with his wife Elizabeth and three children in Northumberland Street Sunderland. All the children had been born in Australia. Elizabeth died in the early 1850s and he remarried an Ann Robinson in Sunderland in 1855 by whom he had three more children. In 1871 he was a wine merchant at 12 Clayton Street Newcastle. In 1881 three of his sons were in the cigar and wine trades. William Glendenning died in Newcastle in 1903 aged 74 (*NDBCC newsletter* 119).

f) No application to register the sword cleaving corn trade mark was found in the *Trade Mark Journals*. Terry Glendenning has told me that the current family assumed that the "sword and corn" trade mark of the firm was a family crest although its origins are unknown (pers. com.). The firm did apply to register a label design for what they described as a sparkling table water named Salzbach on 27 June 1889 (Robertson 2012).

* * *

J. G. Graham, Newcastle

(1) 10oz Hamilton

This rare 10oz blue Hamilton is from a short-lived firm from whom few bottles of any sort have been recorded. It has a conventional blob-top and is embossed on one side as shown with a monogram trade mark of the letters **J. G. G.** along with the proprietor's nam**e J. G. Graham** and **Newcastle**.

J. G. Graham 10oz Hamilton

Notes:

a) J. G. Graham is listed on Westgate Road in Newcastle:
- 1885-1887 James G. Graham, mineral water manufacturer, 160 Westgate Road

b) He is listed as living at 56 Hedley Place in Newcastle in 1887 at which address a G. Graham plumber is listed in 1885.

c) A short note in *The Mineral Water Trade Review and Guardian* July 1885 suggests that the firm started business in 1885:

> Mr J. G. Graham has within the past few weeks entered the ranks of the Newcastle makers, and has pitched his tent in Westgate Road

d) J. G. Graham should not be confused with the more well-known J. H. Graham (John Harper Graham) who was an innkeeper and bottler who built up a large chain of public houses in the North East. This may be why J. G. Graham used his middle initial in the title of his own business.

* * *

James Grieves (& Sons), South Shields

(1) 10oz cylinder (James Grieves)
(2) 6oz cylinder (James Grieves & Sons)

The firm of James Grieves is the first of the two firms from South Shields on the south bank of the River Tyne that are known to have used blue glass mineral water bottles. He used two types of blue cylinder both of which are very rare. Type (1), the 10oz cylinder, is embossed **James Grieves** and **South Shields** along with the firm's trade mark of a sea-serpent with the words **Trade Mark**. There is no maker's mark and the back and base of the bottle are plain. From the dates of the firm's title as detailed below this type dates from 1841-1900.

Type (2) is a 6oz cylinder, a whole example of which only came to light in 2007. The embossing consists of the later firm's title **James Grieves & Sons** and **South Shields** along with the firm's sea-serpent trade mark with the words **Trade Mark**. This example also has the number **4** embossed on the back indicating that it was made by Dan Rylands of Barnsley. The base is embossed **A10**. The A10 mark dates it to post-1891 as detailed in chapter three and we can further pin it down to 1901-1902 which is when trade directories indicate that the firm used the James Grieves & Sons title. Both types of cylinder are illustrated.

 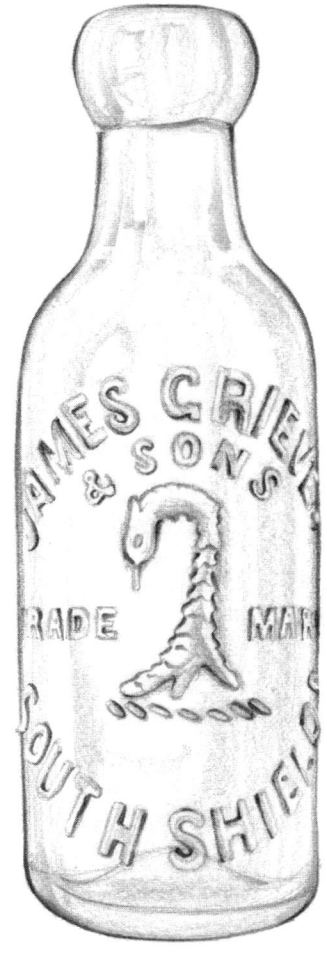

James Grieves 10oz cylinder   James Grieves & Sons 6oz cylinder

Notes:

a) This long-lasting firm is listed in South Shields as a mineral water manufacturer under the following titles:
   - 1841-1900 James Grieves
   - 1901-1902 James Grieves & Sons
   - 1903-1912 Grieves & Co.
   - 1913-1961 Grieves & Co. Ltd

The registered office of the limited company is listed as 25 King St., South Shields with J. T. Reed as secretary 1921-1934.

b) The firm is listed at the following addresses in South Shields:
- 1841 3 Church Way
- 1844-1872 Bottlehill, Bottlebank, East Holborn
- 1876-1877 Coxe Street
- 1879-1961 27 Ingham Street

c) Census returns show that James Grieves was born in South Shields. In 1881, aged 51, he had two sons – John Mathen Grieves and George Mathen Grieves. He is also listed in directories as a grocer, flour and general dealer at Bottlebank 1865; Addisons Place 1865-1866; 148 Eldon Street 1867-1872; 4 Laygate Street 1875-1876 and 97 Eldon Street 1875-1877.

d) James Grieves was part of the consortium that tried (unsuccessfully) to form the Northern Bottle Manufacturing Co. Ltd in 1892 (*NDBCC newsletter* 95).

e) *The Mineral Water Trade Journal* November 1909 reported the formation of a private company:

MESSRS. GRIEVES & CO.

Capital of £4,000. Objects: To take over the business carried on at Ingham- Street, South Shields, as Grieves & Co. Agreement with Messrs. W. Haggart and D. Petrie. Aerated water manufacturers, etc. Private.

f) Grieves & Co. Ltd was acquired by Westoe Breweries Ltd, South Shields in 1949 (Richmond & Turton 1990).

g) James Grieves & Sons, Ingham Street applied to register the words Conio (no. 237,505) and Vesso (no. 237,506) as trade marks for mineral waters in Class 44 on 17 April 1901. Application to register the sea-serpent trademark used on their blue glass mineral water bottles was not found in the *Trade Mark Journals*.

* * *

Hornsby Brothers, Gateshead

(1) 10oz flat-bottomed Hamilton

This is the second of the Gateshead firms who used blue glass mineral water bottles. An example of their previously unrecorded 10oz flat-bottomed blue hamilton was first seen in 2002 and Hornsby Brothers remains a firm from which few bottles of any sort are seen locally. Their blue 10oz flat-bottomed hamilton has a conventional blob-top and is embossed on one side as shown with a stylish monogram of the letters **HB** within a diamond-shaped outline along with the firm's title **Hornsby Bros** and **Gateshead**. There is no maker's mark and the base is plain.

Notes:

a) The firm Hornsby Brothers is unlisted in trade directories.

b) The surname Hornsby appears in Gateshead from the mid-nineteenth century onwards in various trades such as butchers, marine store dealers, grocers, coal merchants and innkeepers but none with an obvious connection to the mineral water trade and none trading as Hornsby Brothers.

* * *

J. Kershaw & Sons, Gateshead

(1) Ginger beer
(2) 10oz four-way patent internal stopper

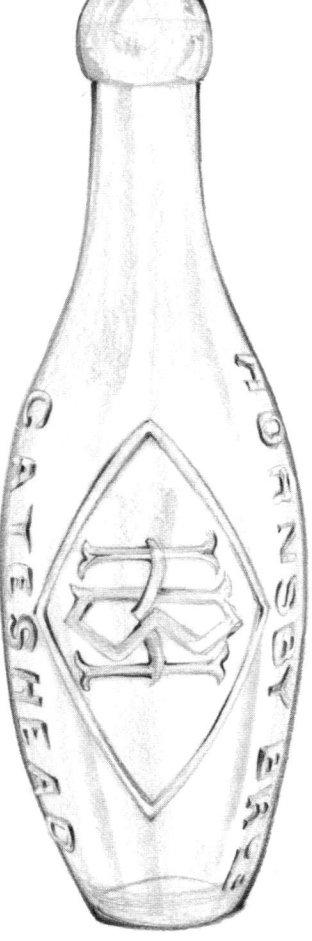

10oz Hornsby Brothers flat-bottomed Hamilton

This well-known and long-lasting mineral water manufacturer is the third firm from Gateshead who used blue glass mineral water bottles. Two types of bottles are known from the firm and both are extremely rare and highly sought-after.

Type (1), the ginger beer, is the only bottle of this shape in the North East blue glass catalogue. The few examples seen have all been a very deep cobalt blue rendering much of the bottle opaque. The bottle is embossed on one side with an attractive design used extensively by the firm on its bottles which consists of the firm's title **J. Kershaw & Sons** and **Gateshead** along with their pictorial trade mark of a bird-in-the-bush and the words **Registered** and **Trade Mark**. The bottle is 8 inches (204mm) high and holds 10oz to the brim. It has no maker's mark and the base and the back are plain. This bottle does not have the contents specified in the embossing but the shape is noted as a glass ginger beer in contemporary advertisements as detailed in chapter two.

Type (2) is a 10oz four-way patent style internal-stopper which is embossed with the same design seen on the ginger beer above. It is the same design as the well-known

Dobson's four-way patent, the familiar aqua version of which is embossed with J. W. Dobson's name and details as the maker. This blue glass version is however embossed on the back **Dan Rylands/ 4/ Makers/ Barnsley**. The stopper is a double-ended glass bobbin with a rubber ring around the middle. J. W. Dobson obtained provisional patent protection for his four-way patent closure on 30 November 1885 (no. 14,693) and so Dan Rylands unattributed use of this closure must date to later than this. Also the change in the firm's name from J. Kershaw to J. Kershaw & Sons and the absence of the word Leadgate in the address, as detailed below, means we can narrow down the date of this bottle to the 1887-1901 period. The lack of the A10 mark, extensively used by Kershaw when introduced, suggests it was pre-1891 as detailed in chapter three. Both types are illustrated.

J. Kershaw & Sons ginger beer

J. Kershaw & Sons Four-Way patent

Notes:

a) The firm is listed as a mineral water manufacturer, ale & porter merchant, wholesale tobacconist, sauce pickle and preserves manufacturer under the titles:
- 1881-1886 James Kershaw (greengrocer and botanic beer maker)
- 1887-1907 J. Kershaw & Sons
- 1907-1964 J. Kershaw & Sons Ltd

b) The firm is listed at the following addresses:
- 1881-1884 Bird-in-the-Bush Yard, 38 Bottle Bank, Gateshead
- 1881-1886 38 Askew Road, Gateshead
- 1887-1964 Back Askew Road, Gateshead
- 1901-1955 Plantation Street, Leadgate, Co. Durham

The firm's Leadgate branch became a permanent named address of the firm at the turn of the century. Leadgate is described in Whellan (1894) as "a large and populous village stretched along the turnpike road between Consett and Dipton thirteen miles south-west of Newcastle".

Advertisement from Ward's Directory of Newcastle & Gateshead etc.1899-1900

c) Different sources give a variety of dates in the history of this firm. The summary below is compiled from *A Descriptive Account of Newcastle: Illustrated* (c.1893), census returns, the Kershaw family tree website, the mineral water trade press and obituaries in *The Mineral Water Trade Journal* April 1906 and the *Newcastle Daily Chronicle* April 1906:

- 1841 James Kershaw born in Askam, Westmoreland
- 1868 Worked in Barrow-in-Furness as an ironworker
- 1871 Married Jane Surgeon of Cotehill
- 1878 Moved to Gateshead (horehound beer dealer Strawberry Lane)
- 1881 Mineral water business founded Bird-in-the-Bush Yard, High Street
- 1881 Residence 38 Askew Road, with his wife and four sons all born in Barrow, Nathan, Henry, John James, William Surgeon and Arthur Robert
- 1883 Bought two blocks of buildings behind Askew Road to use as a factory
- 1892 Town councillor in Gateshead. Prominent in public affairs

- 1892 Third factory extension in seven years, 45ft x 24ft, (stabling, granary, hay-loft)
- 1893 A temperance business making soda water, potass, ginger beer, dandelion stout, Zolacone (Zola nut tonic), lime juice, hop bitters, botanic beer. The firm has fourteen horses and delivers up to 15 miles. Largely run by sons
- 1903 Firm employs 29 people
- 1904 James Kershaw visits the Canary Islands and Capetown
- 1906 James Kershaw died on 31 March
- 1907 J. Kershaw & Sons Ltd registered. Capital £7,000 in £1 shares. To adopt an agreement with Jane Kershaw and J. Ross for the acquisition of the business of mineral water manufacturers, ale, beer, porter, stout and spirit merchant, carried on by them at Gateshead and Leadgate Durham. No initial public issue. Registered without articles of association
- 1908 Firm employs 58 people.
- 1964 Business officially closed in May this year

Engraving from *The Newcastle Daily Chronicle* obituary 2 April 1906

d) James Kershaw was actively involved in the Northumberland and Durham Mineral Water Bottle Exchange and Trade Protection Society Ltd being President and Chairman by 1892. He was also part of the (unsuccessful) attempt to form the Northern Bottle Manufacturing Co. Ltd that year.

e) Despite its initial temperance theme, by 1901 the firm is listed as bottling beer. In 1920 they advertised as "Bottlers of Harp Label Guinness' Stout; Bass's Pale Ale; Regent Sauces and Pickles and High Class Preserves Manufacturers". In 1929 they also advertised as wholesale tobacconists.

Trade mark registration of James Kershaw

f) James Kershaw, 38 Bottle Bank, Gateshead applied to register the bird-in-the-bush device as a trade mark in Class 44 (no. 34,096) on 1 November 1883 with no claim for its use prior to 1875.

* * *

Jas Mckie & Son(s), Newcastle

Jas McKie & Son

Type (1) 6oz cylinder
Type (2) 10oz round-bottomed cylinder
Type (3) 10oz Hamilton
Type (4) 10oz Hamilton (etched)

Jas McKie & Sons

Type (5) 6oz cylinder
Type (6) 10oz round-bottomed cylinder

The well-known firm of James McKie in Newcastle used a range of blue glass mineral waters which have one of two types of embossing. One has the firm's title as Jas McKie & Son and the other as Jas McKie & Sons. None of the six types has a maker's mark.

Types (1) to (4) are embossed **Jas McKie & Son/ Newcastle**. They all have conventional blob-tops and the cylinder has a plain base. The embossed Hamilton, type (3), is the rarest of this group. The type (4) Hamilton has the same wording which is etched (i.e. sandblasted) in a lozenge-shaped design unusually orientated for a Hamilton to be read with the bottle upright. The first and so far only example of this type that I have seen came to light at the National Bottle Show in Yorkshire in 2002 and was also the first etched blue glass mineral seen from the North East. These four types should date to 1887-97 which is the period that directories indicate the firm was using the title Jas McKie & Son. All four types are illustrated.

Types (5) and (6), a 6oz cylinder and a 10oz round-bottomed cylinder, are embossed in three lines **Jas McKie & Sons/ Estd 1835/ Newcastle**. They have conventional blob-tops and the base of the cylinder is plain. They should date to 1898-1917 which is the period that trade directories show the firm used the title Jas McKie & Sons. The claimed establishment date of 1835 is discussed in the notes below. Both of these types are illustrated.

Jas McKie & Son 6oz cylinder

Jas McKie & Son 10oz etched Hamilton

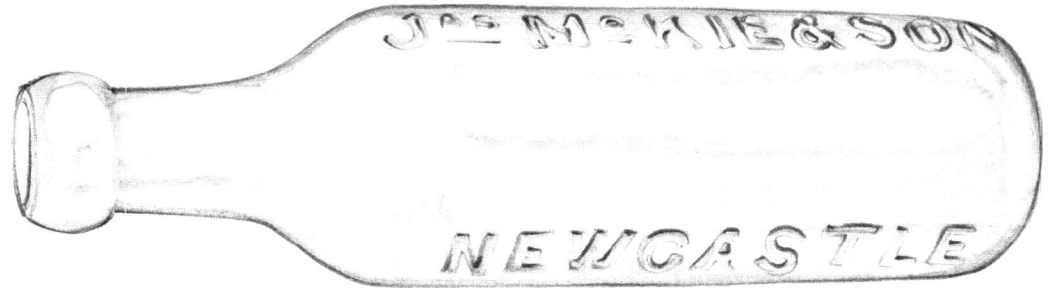
Jas McKie & Son 10oz round-bottomed cylinder

Jas McKie & Son 10oz Hamilton

Jas McKie & Sons 6oz cylinder

Jas McKie & Sons 10oz round-bottomed cylinder

Notes:

a) The firm is listed as a mineral water manufacturer in Newcastle upon Tyne:

- 1847-1862 Dispensary Square, Low Friar Street
- 1863-1890 Bath Road
- 1891-1917 Northumberland Road

Jas McKie & Sons 1912 billhead showing the Northumberland Road premises

The last two addresses above relate to the same location. Bath Road was a section of Northumberland Road where the City Baths were situated. The name Bath Road was dropped around 1890.

b) Proprietors of the firm are listed as:

- 1847-1856 William McKie
- 1857 Brand & McKie (Andrew Brand & William McKie)
- 1858-1876 A. & J. McKie (Alexander & James)
- 1877-1880 James McKie
- 1881-1886 James McKie Junior
- 1887-1897 James McKie & Son (James senior & James junior)
- 1898-1910 James McKie & Sons (Jacob & James)
- 1911-1917 James McKie & Sons (James)

The Mineral Water Trade Review and Guardian August 1877 contains a testimonial for Codd's patent from "A. & W. McKie, 1 Bath Road, Newcastle on Tyne" possibly a misprint as this partnership is not listed in trade directories.

c) The origin of the firm's establishment date of 1835 seen on types (5) and (6) is not clear. The first listing is of a William McKie soda water manufacturer in 1847 as above. The name William McKie does appear in Newcastle at other locations under other trades from 1838 so possibly soda water manufacture was not his first business. No other soda water manufacturers are listed at Dispensary Square prior to 1847.

d) *The Mineral Water Trade Review and Guardian* August 1879 reported under company liquidations that of "J. McKie, 1 Bath Road, Newcastle on Tyne, soda water maker". The same paper in September 1879, January 1880 and April 1881 reported under Bankruptcy Notices that of "J. McKie 1 Bath Road, Newcastle, soda water manufacturer".

e) *The Mineral Water Trade Review and Guardian* May 1873 reported a meeting of North East mineral water manufacturers called by Alexander McKie, as vice-chairman, and J. J. Bell (q.v.) as chairman to initiate the formation of what became the Northumberland & Durham Mineral Water and Ale & Porter Bottle Exchange and Trade Protection Society Ltd.

f) *The Mineral Water Trade Journal* May 1910 reported that "Mr James McKie, mineral water manufacturer, of Northumberland-road, Newcastle left an estate to the value of £3,681".

g) Items in *The Mineral Water Trade Journal* in 1917 support that year as the date when the firm went out of business. In October of that year it reported that "Messrs. Richardson & Co. have purchased all split-Codds, split-boxes and 10-ounce Codds bearing the name J. McKie and Sons Newcastle" and in November that "Mr R. Andison, of Jarrow, has purchased all bottles, boxes and cases bearing the name of James McKie and Sons, Newcastle".

* * *

Newcastle upon Tyne & District Aerated Water Co. Limited

(1) 6oz flat-bottomed Hamilton
(2) 10oz flat-bottomed Hamilton

The Newcastle upon Tyne & District Aerated Water Company Ltd (abbreviated by collectors to "Newcastle & District") used two sizes of flat-bottomed blue Hamiltons which are embossed on both sides and are much sought-after. The firm is also noteworthy for using the full city name, Newcastle upon Tyne, in its title rather than the shortened Newcastle or Newcastle on Tyne.

Types (1) and (2) have the same embossed design. One side of the bottle has the firm's title **Newcastle Upon/ Tyne & District/ Aerated Water/ Co. Limited** in four lines. The other side has the firm's decorative trade mark of the city's coat of arms within a circle along with the words **Trade Mark**. The coat of arms consists of two seahorses flanking a shield bearing three castle turrets and above it a lion rampant against a flagpole and pennant. Neither of the two types has a maker's mark and both have **A10** embossed on the base dating them to post-1891. Both sides of the type (1) are illustrated.

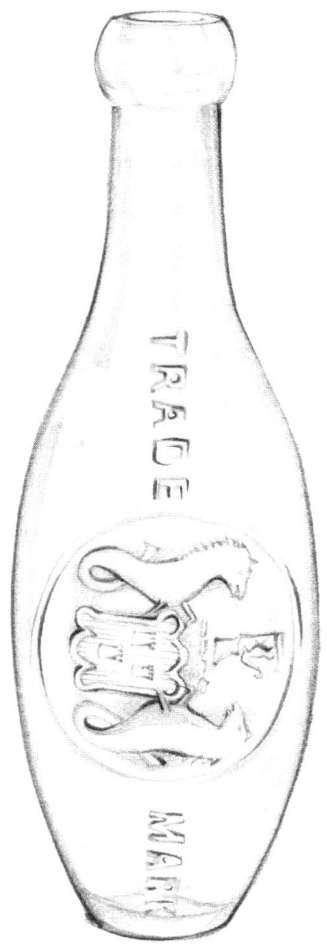 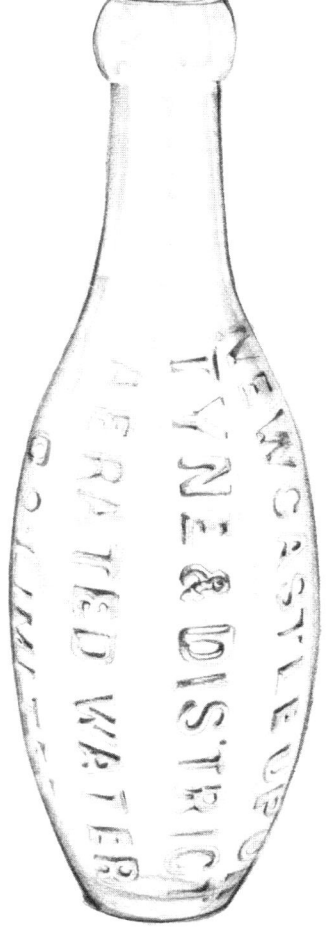

Newcastle & District 6oz flat-bottomed Hamilton Newcastle & District 6oz flat-bottomed Hamilton reverse

Notes:

a) The firm is listed as a mineral water manufacturer in Newcastle as follows:
   - 1889-1909 29 Orchard Street
   - 1889-1901 54 Westgate Road (offices)
   - 1902-1909 Union Assurance Buildings, 40 Westgate Road (offices)

b) The manufactory was on Orchard Street with the Westgate Road premises listed as offices. Prior to 1890 the firm's Orchard Street address was a vinegar factory which backed directly onto part of the surviving medieval Town Wall of Newcastle on the other side of which was the Hanover Square Brewery. This part of the Town Wall was revealed and preserved during demolition of the brewery and associated buildings in 1986 of which there is a good account in the annual publication of the Society of Antiquaries of Newcastle upon Tyne (*Archaelogia Aeliana* 5th series, volume XXI 1993).

c) *A Descriptive Account of Newcastle Illustrated* (c.1894) has a small article on the business of which the following is taken:

Newcastle-on-Tyne Aerated Water Co., Ltd.,
Works: 29 Orchard Street
Registered Offices: 54 Westgate Road
Mr. J. J. Gillespie, chartered accountant, Secretary

The above Company started business as aerated water manufacturers in 1889...the factory at 29 Orchard Street is not over large as aerated water factories go... In addition to the ordinary aerated waters such as potash, soda, seltzer, ginger ale and lemonade, the goods put forward include fermented ginger beer, lime water and hot tom... Any of the foregoing can be supplied either in full bottles, splits or syphons as required. The factory is fully equipped with all the latest plant and amongst the machinery in use we note McEwens's filling apparatus... Hayward and Tyler's machines for filling corked bottles; and a variety of machines for bottle-washing, aerating etc. A separate department is devoted to the preparation of syrups... A special delivery system has been adopted, four suitably constructed vehicles being kept continually on the go.

Trade mark registration of The Newcastle & District Aerated Water Co. Ltd

d) The firm applied to register their trade mark of a device centred on the city's coat of arms in Class 44 (no. 97,583) for mineral and aerated waters on 2 May 1890.
e) *The Mineral Water Trade Journal* June 1909 recorded the voluntary winding up of the business in a *London Gazette* announcement:

Newcastle-upon-Tyne and District Aerated Water Co., Ltd. To be voluntarily wound up. Liquidator: Mr. Thos. Gillespie, C.A., 40 Westgate-road, Newcastle-upon-Tyne.

* * *

W. B. Reid & Co. Ltd, Newcastle

(1) 6oz cylinder (A A & Co)
(2) 10oz cylinder (A A & Co)
(3) 10oz cylinder (R B B)

Three types of blue glass cylinders are known from the major Newcastle brewing concern of W. B. Reid & Co. Ltd from two different makers. They all have the same embossed design which consists of the firm's registered trade mark of a hand holding an open book inside a garter bearing the words *Pro Virtue* with the firm's title **W. B. Reid & Co. Ld** and the city name **Newcastle**.

Types (1) and (2), a 6oz and a 10oz cylinder, both have **A A & Co** embossed on the lower back which is the maker's mark of the Blaydon on Tyne and Leeds glassmakers of A. Alexander & Co. making them rare examples of North East blue glass mineral water bottles with a known locally-based maker. They both have **A10** embossed on the base showing them to be post-1891.

Type (3), a 10oz cylinder, has the letters **R B B** embossed on the bottom edge of the body indicating that it was made by Redfearn Brothers of Barnsley. It is also embossed **A10** on the base. This type first came to light in 2001 when a tip was discovered during development of a site in Gosforth just north of Newcastle upon Tyne and two examples are known to have been found there both a deep cobalt colour. Types (1) and (3) are both illustrated.

Notes:
a) W. B. Reid & Co. Ltd is listed as a brewer and maltster, wine spirit ale and porter merchant, mineral water manufacturer and innkeeper. The firm's complex history is inseparable from that of two other firms, C. B. Reid & Co. and Reid Brothers &

Co., both in the same trades and both of which also operated in Newcastle upon Tyne. Their shared main addresses in Newcastle are listed together below for ease of reference:

- 1847-1959 Leazes Brewery, Upper Claremont
- 1855-1857 5 New Bridge Street
- 1858-1860 37 Pilgrim Street
- 1861-1864 6 Neville Street
- 1865-1868 2 St Nicholas's Buildings
- 1869-1872 High Bridge
- 1869-1923 53 Grey Street
- 1924-1956 The Leazes, Upper Claremont

W. B. Reid & Co. Ltd 6oz cylinder type (1)

W. B. Reid & Co. Ltd 10oz cylinder type (3)

The second to fourth addresses are listed under ale & porter merchants and agents' offices with the final three addresses under brewers' agents, wine & spirit merchants and offices.

b) W. B. Reid & Co. Ltd advertised a founding date of 1837 for the Leazes Brewery. The listings show a Newcastle Joint Stock Brewery Co. at Upper Claremont 1838-1844 with an Edward Reid as manager 1838-1841. The brewery was subsequently titled Leazes Brewery under C. B. Reid and W. B. Reid (see below).

c) The various family companies in the Reid brewing and bottling empire are dealt with below.

C. B. Reid & Co.

Founded by Christian Bruce Reid. He is listed in 1838 as a goldsmith and other Reid family members formed the well-known Newcastle goldsmiths Reid Brothers. The company is listed in Newcastle:

- 1847-1868 Brewers, Leazes brewery
- 1855-1872 Agents to brewers and wine & spirit merchants

Brewers' agencies are advertised at the main addresses (apart from High Bridge) for the Burton Brewery Co. (Burton on Trent), Findlater & Co. (Dublin) and A. Melvin (Edinburgh) plus the wine & spirit merchant James Gray & Son (Edinburgh). C. B. Reid is also listed as Belgian Consul 1853-1868 and as a partner in W. B. Reid & Co. 1859-1889 and Reid Brothers & Co. 1871-1889. In 1890 his name is unlisted with only his wife at their residence.

W. B. Reid & Co.

Founded by William Bruce Reid (eldest son of C. B. Reid) this company is listed in Newcastle:

- 1853-1959 Brewers, Leazes Brewery
- 1863-1891 Offices at Neville Street, St Nicholas' Buildings and Grey Street

W. B. Reid is also listed as a partner in C. B. Reid & Co. 1859-1874 and in Reid Brothers & Co. 1871-1890. W. B. Reid himself died in 1918 aged 85 (Bennison 2004).

Reid Brothers & Co.

This company is listed in Newcastle:

- 1869-1872 Wine & spirit merchants, High Bridge and Grey Street
- 1873-1891 Brewers' agents, Grey Street

Brewers' agencies were the same as advertised under C. B. Reid & Co. plus an agency for Wm. Younger & Co. (Edinburgh) from 1875. Both C. B. Reid and W. B. Reid are listed as partners in Reid Brothers & Co.

C. K. & W. B. Reid & Co.

Christian Ker Reid became part of the concerns from 1858-1874 in a fourth company C. K. and W. B. Reid & Co. listed from 1867-1871 and other family members appear in the businesses. Thomas Reid (from 1858) and James Reid (from 1873) are listed in the ale & porter agency side of the businesses, the former also being Belgian Vice-Consul in 1863 when C. B. Reid was the Consul. This curious diplomatic core connection was continued by a George Reid who was Belgian Consul from 1871. In *Northumberland at the Opening of the 20th Century* (Pike 1905) there are biographies of Christian Leopold Reid and George Reid, the Reid family goldsmiths business history and the longstanding family connection as Belgian Consuls. Edmund Reid and Edwin Octavious Reid are listed in the 1880s in Reid Brothers & Co., the latter also in W. B. Reid & Co.

W. B. Reid & Co. Ltd

The rationalisation of the business empire came with the registration of W. B. Reid & Co. Ltd in 1891 to acquire W. B. Reid & Co. (Leazes Brewery); Reid Brothers & Co. (wine & spirit merchants); the public houses of the Tyne Brewery Co. Ltd and the agency of William Younger & Co. Ltd for Northumberland and the northern division of Durham. The purchase price was fixed at £263,500 and the share capital was £150,000 and £150,000 of 5% debentures (*Mineral Water Trade Recorder* 1 June 1891). W. B. Reid & Co. Ltd was eventually taken over by Wm. Younger & Co. Ltd in 1956 with 156 public houses. The latter was part of Scottish Brewers Ltd which merged with Newcastle Breweries Ltd in 1960 to bring the firm back to the North East as Scottish & Newcastle Breweries Ltd (Norman Barber 2005).

Advertisement from Kelly's Directory of Northumberland 1902

d) In summary the overall picture is of C. B. Reid starting the business at the Leazes Brewery c. 1847. The name of W. B. Reid &

Co. appears here in the mid-1850s at which time C. B. Reid & Co. concentrated on the brewers' agency and wine & spirit agency side of the business until this became Reid Brothers & Co. around 1871. Apart from C. B. Reid and W. B. Reid several other Reid family members were involved in the complex interrelated family companies. The businesses were merged with the formation of W. B. Reid & Co. Ltd in 1891.

e) The firm advertised mineral water manufacture from 1899. *The Mineral Water Trade Journal* May 1903 noted that the manufactory was at Leazes i.e. at the brewery reporting that:

Mr. Brown who manages the mineral water department of Messrs. Reid at Newcastle, always strikes one as being on good terms with himself. It's not often you see a twinkling eye and enlarging corpulency unless the carrier of this adipose tissue is of a contented mind. He keeps the factory in fine order; his syrup room is a treat and every department bears evidence of intelligent supervision.

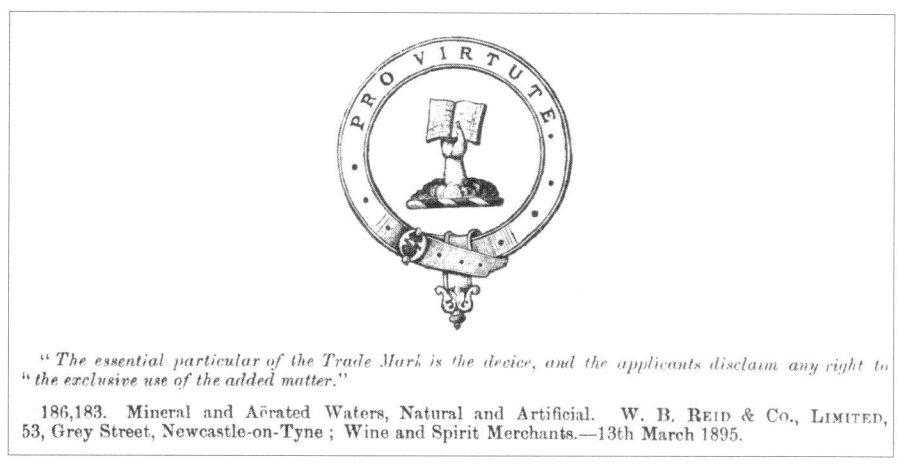

Trade mark registration of W. B. Reid & Co. Ltd

f) Both *Tyneside Industries* (1889) and *A Descriptive Account of Newcastle* (c1894) have articles on W. B. Reid & Co. Ltd and Reid Brothers & Co. from which the following additional material is compiled:

Reid Brothers & Co., wine & spirit merchants was established 1867. It is situated at 53 Grey Street which has a 50ft frontage extending 110ft into High Bridge. There are bonded warehouses on the Close. They are the sole local consignees of Wm. Younger & Co. Ltd. Leazes brewery is worked on the gravitation principle and its ales are popularly known as "Newcastle Mild Ales".

W. B. Reid & Co. Ltd. (in 1894) consists of a chairman and managing director William Bruce Reid, a deputy chairman Alexander Low Bruce (deputy chairman of Wm. Younger & Co. Ltd. Edinburgh) and Mr G. R. Brewis, Mr J. Gordon Morrison (also secretary), Mr E. O. Reid, Mr Henry George Younger (of Wm. Younger & Co. Ltd) as directors.

g) W. B. Reid & Co. Ltd applied to register the trade mark of "a hand holding a book and a garter bearing the words Pro Virtue" in Class 44 (no. 186,183) for mineral and aerated waters on 13 March 1895.

* * *

William Robson, Sunderland

(1) 10oz champagne shape

William Robson champagne

William Robson is the first of the two firms from Sunderland that are known to have used blue glass mineral water bottles and he used the only champagne-shaped mineral water in the North East blue glass catalogue. I have classified it as a 10oz capacity although it actually holds only 9oz to the brim. It is often referred to locally as a beer although its shape is equally applicable to mineral waters and on balance I think as a bottle made of blue glass it was more likely to have held a mineral water than beer. The top has an internal screw-thread for a screw-stopper and is the only such closure seen on a blue glass mineral water bottle from the North East.

The embossing is an oval design in the style of a label which was regularly used by the firm. It encloses the firm's title and address **Wm. Robson Middle St. Sunderland** and the centre has the firm's trade mark of a sextant along with the words **Registered** and **Trade Mark**. The base on all examples seen has the **A10** mark embossed in the centre with **1892** below it and the maker's initials **B & Co Ltd K** above it. The maker is Bagley & Co. Ltd Knottingley in Yorkshire and this base layout with various numbers under the A10 mark is common from this glass bottle maker but it is a curious coincidence that the number 1892 in this case is also the year that the A10 mark was effectively introduced. The bottle itself should date to post-1898 when Bagley & Co. Ltd was registered as a limited company as detailed in chapter one.

James Grieves 10oz cylinder Type (1)

James Grieves & Sons 6oz cylinder Type (2)

Hornsby Bros. 10oz flat-bottomed Hamilton

J. Kershaw & Sons Ginger Beer

Jas Mckie & Son 6oz Cylinder Type (1)   Jas Mckie & Sons 6oz Cylinder Type (5)

Jas Mckie & Son 10oz Hamilton Type (3)

F. Bradford 10oz Hamilton Type (2)

Newcastle & District Aerated Water Co. 10oz flat-bottomed Hamilton

Newcastle & District Aerated Water Co. 10oz flat-bottomed Hamilton – reverse

W. B. Reid & Co. Ltd 10oz cylinder Type (2)   W. B. Reid & Co. Ltd 10oz cylinder Type (3)

Wm Robson Champagne

Ross & Co. 10oz flat-bottomed Hamilton

W. Roome 10oz Hamilton

W. Roome 10oz Hamilton – reverse

Wm Row 10oz round-bottomed cylinder

Wm Row 10oz round-bottomed cylinder – reverse

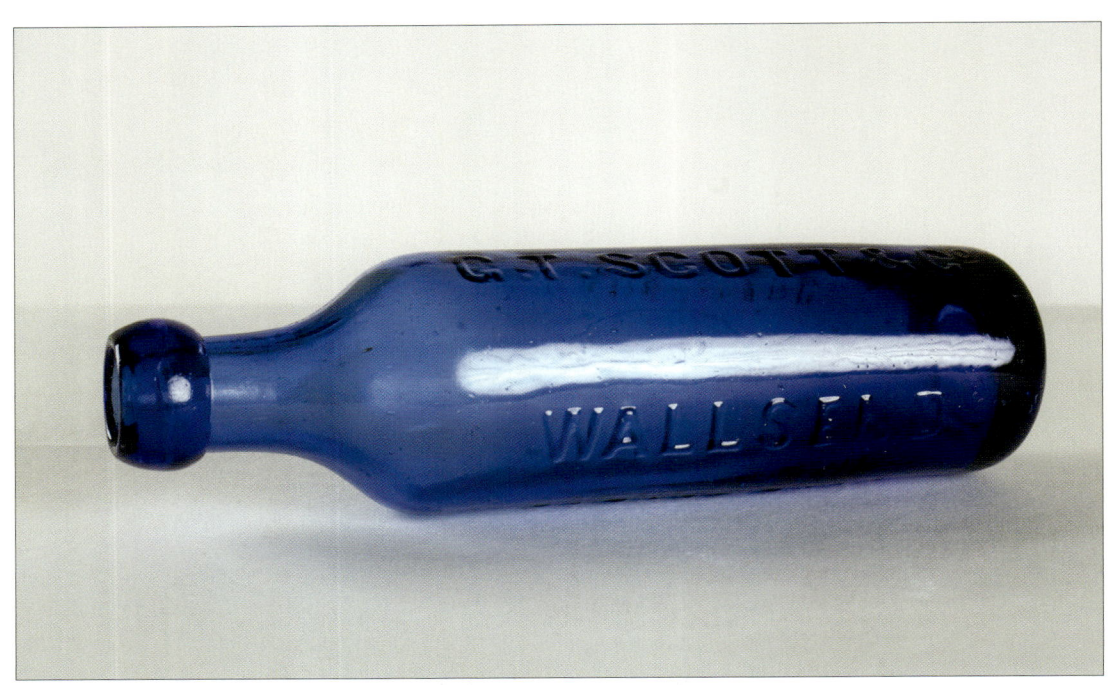

G. T. Scott & Co. 10oz round-bottomed cylinder

G. T. Scott & Co. 10oz round-bottomed cylinder – reverse

Shimmin skittle Codd (Restored)

R. Stephenson 10oz Codd (Restored)

E. J. Stewart 6oz Codd Type (1)

P. Thornton 10oz cylinder Type (1)

Notes:

a) The firm is listed as a wholesale ale & porter merchant and bottler; brewer and mineral water manufacturer at the following addresses:
- 1861-1865 Pan Lane, Sunderland
- 1869-1968 36 Middle Street, Sunderland

b) Titles of the firm are listed as:
- 1861-1875 Spensley & Robson
- 1876-1918 William Robson (Mrs Annie Robson proprietor 1886-1900)
- 1921-1951 William Robson Ltd
- 1954-1968 William Robson (Brewers) Ltd

Until 1876 William Robson was in partnership with a John Spensley trading as Spensley and Robson ale & porter merchants. In 1865 William Robson was living at 19 King Street and from 1869 at 36 and 37 Middle Street.

c) The main listing from 1861-1918 is as an ale & porter merchant and mineral water manufacturer. Mineral water manufacture is first listed in 1874 (under Spensley & Robson) and thereafter until 1968. Brewing is listed from 1901.

d) *The Mineral Water Trade Review and Guardian* September 1879 reported a visit to this firm from which the following is extracted:

> The concern is said to have been in existence about twenty years. The extensive premises extend from Prince Street back to South Street. William Robson himself was averse to modern labour saving devices saying that "Yes that is the way which has ruined the country" and he would not lay off staff that their introduction would cause. The current machinery had been in place some 20 years. Four years previously he employed 70 women and 40 men but now only 14 women and 12 men. The two branches of the firm (mineral water manufacture and beer bottling) were worked completely separately and corks only are used.

William Robson advertisement from the Sunderland Year Book 1910

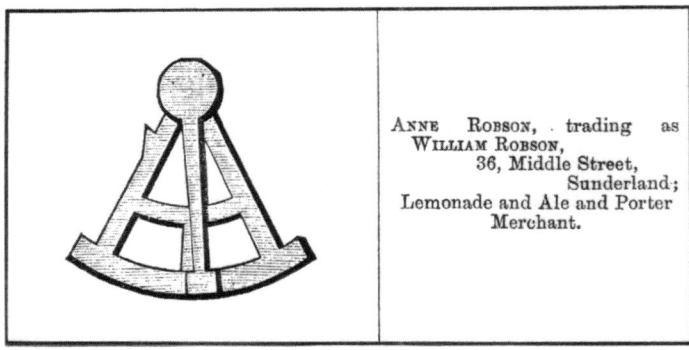

Trade mark registration of William Robson

e) Anne Robson (proprietor from 1886) trading as William Robson applied to register the sextant device as a trade mark in Class 44 (no. 55,962) on 17 August 1886 with no claim of prior use before 1875.

f) William Robson Ltd was registered in 1920 with £40,000 capital to take over the business of brewer and maltster formerly carried on by G. Dove and J. J. Wilson at Middle Street trading as William Robson (Bennison 2004).

g) In the Second World War the Central Brewery at Middle Street was badly damaged by bombing and closed. The company moved to High Street East and continued solely as bottlers. The Robson family ran the concern until 1953 when they sold out to the London wine shippers Adams & Sons Ltd (Archie Miles: unpublished manuscript).

* * *

W. Roome, Darlington

(1) 10oz Hamilton

William Roome of Darlington is the only firm from this important town known to have used a blue glass mineral water bottle and his 10oz blue Hamilton was unrecorded before a deep blue example came to light at the end of 2013. It has a conventional blob-top and is embossed on one side with the name of the proprietor **W. Roome** and on the other side with the town name which is embossed **Dailington** (Darlington). There is, of course, a spelling mistake in the third letter of the name of the town. From the firm's chronology shown below the bottle should date to the 1876-99 period. Both sides of the bottle are illustrated.

W. Roome 10oz Hamilton

W. Roome 10oz Hamilton reverse

Notes:

a) William Roome is listed as a licensed victualler, soda & mineral water manufacturer and beer retailer in Darlington at the following addresses:
   - 1876-1897 18 Upper Archer Street
   - 1881-1894 Brittania Inn, 1 Archer Street
   - 1896-1899 Temperance Place and Four Riggs
   - 1896-1899 37 Larchfield Street

b) *The Mineral Water Trade Review and Guardian* August 1877 noted that William Roome was "residing in Archer Street" when it reported a court case of embezzlement from the firm.

c) Mineral water manufacture is listed at the Upper Archer Street and Temperance Place addresses. Beer retailing is listed at the Larchfield Street address which is also listed as William Roome's residence in the period in question.

d) The business was continued by W. & H. Roome from c.1900.

e) *The Mineral Water Journal* May 1916 reported the death of Mrs S. A. Roome of Darlington:

> We regret to have to record the death of Mrs. S. A. Roome, the widow of the late Mr William Roome who for so many years carried on business as a mineral water manufacturer at Darlington. She was buried at the West Cemetery, Darlington.

f) On stoneware William Roome used a masonic device as a trade mark which can still be seen on the Masonic Hall at Four Riggs today. Application to register it as a trade mark was not found in the *Trade Mark Journals*.

* * *

Ross & Co., Newcastle

(1) 6oz flat-bottomed Hamilton
(2) 10oz flat-bottomed Hamilton

Both of these flat-bottomed blue Hamiltons from Ross & Co. are rare. They are broader based and more stable than the more familiar North East type of flat-bottomed Hamiltons. Their shape is akin to that of the Bradford Brothers Newcastle type (3) and the Gilpin & Co., Newcastle type (6). The base of the 10oz Ross & Co. is $1\frac{7}{8}$ inches (47mm) across and is plain. The 6oz type has the letter **A** embossed on the base. Both types have the same embossed design of the firm's trade mark of a rampant lion and the words **Trade Mark** in between **Ross & Co.** and **Newcastle**. Neither type has a maker's mark. They must date to post-1900 as this was the year that the company's name was first used in Newcastle as detailed below. The 10oz size type (2) is illustrated.

Notes:

a) Ross & Co. is listed as a mineral water manufacturer and ale & porter merchant:
- 1900-1918 1 George Street, Newcastle upon Tyne
- 1900-1912 Delves Lane, Consett, Co. Durham

Ross & Co. 10oz flat-bottomed Hamilton

b) In 1900 James Deuchar acquired the well-known firms of R. Emmerson Junior 1 George Street Newcastle and Nathan Elsdon Delves Lane Consett in County Durham. Both firms were flourishing mineral water manufacturers and ale & porter bottlers and Deuchar continued them both under the name of Ross & Co. the name being transferred from William Ross & Co. of the Lochside Brewery in Montrose, Tayside which James Deuchar had also acquired. There was, at this time, a considerable local demand in the north of England for both Scottish and Burton pale ales and James Deuchar's acquisition of a Scottish brewery to ship his own Scottish Ales (Lochside Ales) to Newcastle was a good business move.

c) At Delves Lane Consett the name Ross & Co. was used until 1912 after which the address is unlisted. At the George Street Newcastle manufactory, which is where these flat-bottomed blue Hamiltons are presumed to have been filled, the name Ross & Co. was used until 1918. From 1919 the Ross & Co. title is dropped and was replaced with J. Deuchar Ltd mineral water manufacturer until the manufactory was closed in 1929.

d) The rampant lion trade mark seen on these Ross & Co. Newcastle flat-bottomed blue Hamiltons was originally used by William Ross at his Montrose Brewery. James Deuchar became the official subsequent proprietor of the well-known penny-farthing trade mark (no. 73,842 Class 43) of R. Emmerson Junior and was registered as such in the *Trade Mark Journal* period for 28 November to 4 December 1901. He also used the penny-farthing trade mark on stone stout bottles (Doctor's Stout) under the Ross & Co. name, no doubt to trade on its popularity from R. Emmerson Junior's time.

* * *

William Row, Newcastle
(1) 6oz round-bottomed cylinder
(2) 10oz round-bottomed cylinder

The well-known Newcastle firm of William Row used two types of blue round-bottomed cylinders both of which are highly desirable.

Type (1) is a 6oz size and the only example I've seen consists of the bottom half only. The embossing is very prominent and reads on one side **(Wm) Row/ (Manufa)cturer/ (Newcastl)e on Tyne** in three rows and on the other side the firm's trade mark of a reposed lion with the words **(Regis)tered** above and **(Trade) Mark** below.

Type (2), the 10oz blue round-bottomed cylinder, is better known. It is embossed on one side in three lines **Wm. Row/ Manufacturer/ Newcastle on Tyne** as on the 6oz

William Row 10oz round-bottomed cylinder

William Row 10oz round-bottomed cylinder reverse

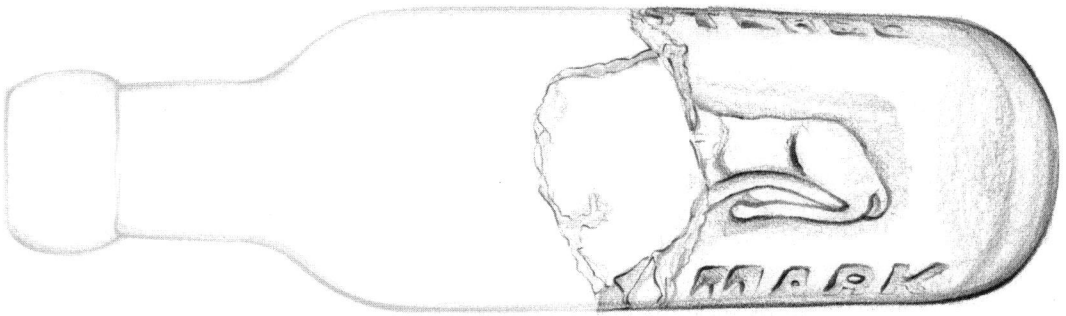
William Row 6oz round-bottomed cylinder

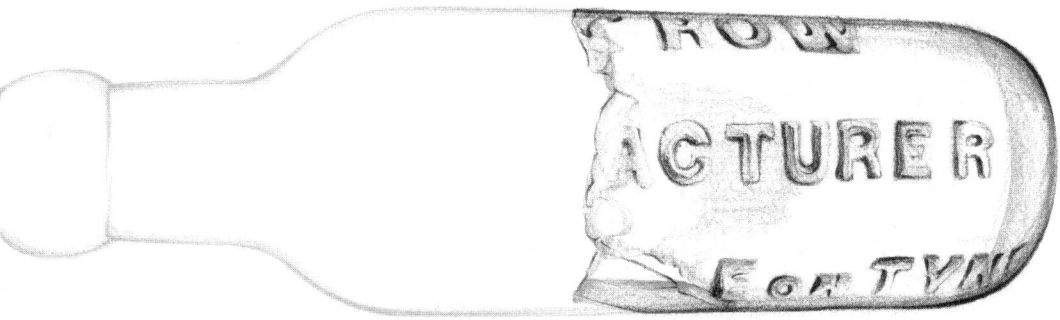
William Row 6oz round-bottomed cylinder reverse

example and on the other side the reposed lion trade mark with the words **Trade Mark** underneath it. The word Registered above the trade mark as seen on the 6oz example is not present on the 10oz example. The difference in the embossing on the two types raises the possibility of two other versions – a 6oz version without the word Registered and a 10oz version with the word Registered although at the time of writing I have not seen examples of either. Both sides of the incomplete 6oz size and the complete 10oz size are illustrated.

Notes:

a) The 1881 census records that William Row, born in Newcastle upon Tyne, was a tripe preparer, aged 40, living at Low Friar Street with his wife Mary (tripe preparer), son John B. (tripe preparer), daughters Margaret (dressmaker) and Hannah (scholar), John Hepple (father-in-law, shoemaker), Mary Thewell (servant) and Thomas Charlton (cartman).

b) William Row is listed at the following addresses in Newcastle:
   - 1869-1894 Fenkle Street
   - 1875-1894 Low Friar Street
   - 1873-1874 Sadlers Well Public House, 18 Low Friar Street
   - 1877-1894 84 Market
   - 1883-1894 Radcliffe's Court, Stowell Street
   - 1883-1888 Northumberland Arms Inn, Stowell Street

c) He is listed under a variety of occupations – a steam tripe dresser, a neats foot oil & tallow merchant, a mineral water manufacturer, an ale porter wine and cigar merchant and a licensed victualler as follows:
   - William Row's tripe and tallow chandlers business was at the Fenkle Street, Low Friar Street and Market addresses. His son, John Burnett Row, tripe preparer, was also listed here from 1861-76 with Fenkle Street and Low Friar Street as his home. William Row was resident at Low Friar Street 1875-94. The Fenkle Street and Low Friar Street addresses were re-numbered in 1883 being number 7 and 14 respectively before that date and 15 and 24 thereafter.
   - The Market was, and still is, a substantial permanent indoor market in Newcastle situated between Grainger Street, Clayton Street, Nun Street and Nelson Street. It was opened in 1835.
   - The mineral water manufactory and ale & porter business is listed only at Radcliffe's Court on Stowell Street. Low Friar Street and Stowell Street are in the historic medieval Black Friars precinct of Newcastle where the ancient

trade companies were once based and there is an interesting, and relevant, history of this area in *Archaelogia Aeliana Fifth Series vol. XV 1987 p.23*.

- The Sadler's Wells and the Northumberland Arms Inn are the only two public houses listed under William Row's name in Newcastle.

g) *Rivers of the North* (1894) has a promotional article on the firm from which the following is an edited summary:

William Row,
Wholesale Wine, Ale, and Porter Merchant, Cigar Dealer, and Mineral Water Manufacturer, Stowell Street, Newcastle-on-Tyne

Mr. William Row…in the year 1880 acquired the thriving business which had been organised by a Mr. Edward Jardine as far back as 1840. The records of the business show that its commercial development has been both rapid and continuous from the commencement. The premises…consist of an extensive two-storey building admirably constructed as a store for choice wines of all the best brands, ales and porters – notably the ales of Messrs. Bass & Co. and Worthington & Co. and D'Arcy's Dublin stout for all of which Mr. Row is the special local agent; and mineral waters and aerated drinks of every kind which are manufactured on the premises – the mineral water plant…being driven by gas power. On the upper floor Mr. Row manufactures all kinds of choice cordials; and he holds large stores and stables for a good service of horses and delivery vans on the opposite side of the street.

h) Trade directory listings and advertisements give a more detailed early history of the bottling business that William Row eventually acquired:

- 1859-1864 Edward Amory Jardine, ale & porter merchant, 14 Portland Place, New Bridge Street
- 1865-1878 Edward Amory Jardine, ale & porter merchant, Stowell Street
- 1879-1880 John Hall, soda water manufacturer, Stowell Street
- 1881-1882 Mrs I. S. Hall, soda water manufacturer, Stowell Street

John Hall advertised in 1879 that he had "succeeded to the business so successfully carried on for nearly 20 years by Mr E. A. Jardine" (which confirms the establishment date as 1859 rather than 1840 as given in *Rivers of the North*).

i) William Row was part of the consortium of North East bottlers who

Trade mark registration of William Row

tried (unsuccessfully) in 1892 to form a Northern Bottle Manufacturing Co. Ltd (*NDBCC newsletter* no. 95).

j) The year 1894 seems to be William Row's last one in business. In 1895 W. Simpson is listed at the tripe-preparing addresses with Dover, McEwan & Co. (brewer) as a mineral water manufacturer at the Radcliffe's Court Stowell Street address.

k) William Row applied to register a reposed lion with the letter R on its flank as a trade mark in Class 44 (no. 56,350) for mineral and aerated waters on 2 September 1886 with no use of the device claimed prior to 1875.

* * *

G. T. Scott & Co. Wallsend

(1) 6oz cylinder
(2) 10oz cylinder

G. T. Scott & Co. from Wallsend on the north bank of the River Tyne is the only firm from the town known to have used blue glass for a mineral water bottle. With its celebrated trade mark of Father Tyne the firm is a well-known to local collectors. It used two types of blue cylinders both of which are attractive and rare. The embossed design is the same on both types and consists of **G. T. Scott & Co.** and **Wallsend** in two lines on one side and on the other side the firm's trade mark of Father Tyne with the words **Father Tyne** above and **Trade Mark** below. The bases on both types are plain and neither type has a maker's mark. The 6oz type (1) has a more pronounced shoulder than the 10oz type (2) and both sides of both types are illustrated.

Notes:

a) The proprietor of the business was George Thorpe Scott and he is listed in trade directories as a beer retailer, innkeeper, mineral water manufacturer and bottler:
- 1879-1884 Beer retailer, High Street, Wallsend
- 1885-1894 Queen's Head Inn, 58 High Street, Wallsend
- 1891-1894 60 High Street, Wallsend

G.T. Scott & Co 10oz cylinder

| G.T. Scott & Co 10oz cylinder reverse | G.T. Scott & Co 6oz cylinder reverse | G.T. Scott & Co 6oz cylinder |

b) Trade directories name a William Fletcher at The Queen's Head Inn 58 High Street in 1879 but do not use the pub's name again until 1885 when it was under Scott. Census returns however name G. T. Scott there in 1881 hence this may have been his address since 1879-80.

c) The 60 High Street address is listed as G. T. Scott & Co.'s mineral water works

d) G. T. Scott was born in 1855 at Rainton Mill, East Rainton, County Durham, the son of a farmer and corn-miller John Scott who is named in 1871 in Gateshead as an auctioneer and ale & porter merchant with George as a storekeeper. G. T. Scott married Elizabeth Sutherland in Gateshead in 1873. In 1881 he is recorded as a beer-house keeper at the Queen's Head, High Street West, Wallsend with his wife and four children and in 1891 as a mineral water manufacturer. In 1901, living at Byker, he is recorded as a public house manager (*NDBCC newsletter* no 118, September 2007).

e) *A Descriptive Account of Newcastle, Illustrated* (c.1894) has an article on the business written in 1893 from which the following is taken:

Mr. G.T. Scott,
Aerated Water Manufacturer & Bottler of Bass's Ales,
60 High Street, Wallsend

Its establishment dates to...1891...only two years ago with one solitary man, one woman and one boy (G. T. Scott attending to the outdoor and clerical business). The firm now keep a staff of twelve indoor hands with three horses...delivering goods... and collecting bottles, syphons etc. from...a radius of several miles.

The building was once the church of a Presbyterian congregation...the edifice was purchased by Mr. Scott and equipped with aerated water plant by Messrs Galloway... Bolton ...motor power being supplied by steam engine and boiler.

Mr. Scott procures gas ready prepared by a Clapham (London) firm in wrought iron tubes. Specialities...include...soda, potass water etc., lemonade, cider and hop ale. We commend to our readers Mr. Scott's "Fermented Ginger Beer". Essences...are made by his foreman Mr. George Brown. The firm also engage in bottling Messrs. Bass & Co.'s ales, Messrs. James Muir & Co. Edinburgh ales and Messrs. Guinness & Co's Dublin Stout.

f) The above is good evidence that whilst retailing beer at 58 High Street he bought the next door church at number 60 in 1891 and converted it into a mineral water works and bottling plant. *A History of the Parish of Wallsend* (Richardson 1923) notes that a Presbyterian church was built on the south side of High Street West in 1823 with galleries round three sides and square pews to seat 250 which could be the church converted by G. T. Scott.

Trade mark registration of G. T. Scott

g) G. T. Scott applied to register his well-known trade mark of an engraving of Father Tyne in Class 44 (no. 154,741) for mineral and aerated waters on 11 March 1891.

The River God of the Tyne (Father Tyne) was used as a trade mark through the years by a variety of Newcastle publishers including M. A. Richardson, Andrew Reid and latterly Frank Graham. Originally a sculpture outside of Somerset House in 1786 there is a detailed engraving of it by J. Fittler in John Brand's *History & Antiquities of Newcastle* of 1789 (*Historic Newcastle:* Frank Graham, Newcastle 1976).

h) From 1895-96 the firm of A. L. Glendenning & Co., mineral water manufacturer, is listed at 60 High Street with G. T. Scott as a fruiterer at 55 High Street & Clyde Street and a William Hall Newham at the Queen's Head Inn 58 High Street. Glendenning continued to use the Father Tyne trade mark although no blue glass bottles are known from his business.

* * *

Shimmin, Sunderland

(1) 6oz Skittle Codd (flat-bottomed Codd-hamilton hybrid)

This is the second of the two firms from Sunderland known to have used blue glass mineral water bottles and Shimmin's legendary bottle exists as a single example missing its top. Many collectors will not have seen it although it was on display for many years in the bottle shop in Alston Cumbria run by pioneering North East bottle collector and antique dealer the late Arthur Rowlands. Known locally as "King Arthur" he was one of the hobby's early characters and his hospitality and collections always made the long trip up to Alston worthwhile for North East collectors in the 1970s and 1980s.

Many years after he closed his original bottle shop Arthur allowed me to catalogue his fine collection of North East stone stout and ginger beer bottles at his home in Alston. His old cottage was an Aladdin's Cave of collectables and antiques and I hoped I might see the blue Codd as well. He had no idea where it was which was understandable in the chaos of boxes, chests and furniture that filled his house from top to bottom, some rooms of which could not even be entered being filled up to the door. The job was not made easier by the lack of any electricity outlets in most of the house and the choice was either using a bare light bulb on a very long piece of flex or feeling around in the dark with a torch which is how I eventually, by luck, came upon this bottle in a box of odds and ends. The shape, even at the bottom of a box in the dark, was unmistakable and certainly raised my heart-rate when I grasped it! Arthur, being the man he was, happily let me photograph it and the photographs appeared in the *NDBCC newsletter* no. 28 in March 1985 to establish its authenticity.

There have been many stories about the source of this item and I can only repeat what Arthur told me which was that it was in a box of bottles brought into his shop in the mid 1970s by a digger who said that he had dug it in the Roker area of Sunderland although other reliable sources suggest it came from a long dug-out site near Boldon. It was topless when found.

As detailed in chapter two this bottle is a flat-bottomed Codd-Hamilton hybrid that is locally called a Skittle Codd, a name I have stayed with. It has now been restored and as such is 7½ inches (191mm) high, the same height as an average 6oz Codd. It is embossed on the front **Shimmin** and **Sunderland** around the date **1903**. The maker's name is embossed lowdown on the back and reads **Dobson & Nall Ltd/ Bottle & Cask Makers/ Barnsley**. The base of the bottle is 1¼ inches (31mm) across and is plain. No further examples are known although aqua examples of the same size, also topless, have been seen with 1902 and 1903 dates on them (N*DBCC newsletter* issue 65 1994). The bottle is illustrated as originally found.

Shimmin Skittle Codd

Notes:

a) The firm's proprietor, George Shimmin, is listed under various occupations and the chronology below is compiled from trade directories, the *Sunderland Year Book*, trade press advertisements and records of court hearings:

- 1883-1888 secretary, 12 Rosslyn Terrace, Sunderland
- 1889-1890 secretary, 36 Fawcett Street, Sunderland
- 1891-1902 accountant & valuer, (32) 36 Fawcett Street, Sunderland
- 1899-1909 accountant & valuer, 20 Bridge Street, Sunderland
- 1902-1907 mineral water manufacturer, 17 Burnville Road, Sunderland
- 1905-1906 electroplater, Burnville Road, Sunderland

b) The Fawcett Street address is variously numbered as 32, 32 & 36 or 36. George Shimmin was a successful valuer, estate agent and building society secretary and William MacDonald's *An Illustrated Guide to Sunderland and District* (Edinburgh & London 1898) has a short promotional article on the firm from which the following is taken:

George Shimmin
Licensed Valuer and Estate Agent
20 Bridge Street
Sunderland

Mr. Shimmin commenced practice in Sunderland about seventeen years ago... The class of business includes...valuer's work, estate, land and property agency and rent collecting. Amongst the offices held are...the secretaryship of the Sunderland Neptune Permanent Building Society; Sunderland 339th Starr-Bowkett Building Society; 2nd Sunderland 417th Starr-Bowkett Building Society; 3rd Sunderland 536th Starr-Bowkett Building Society; 4th Sunderland 937th Starr-Bowkett Building Society; 1st and 2nd Sunderland Paragon Building Societies; the Sunderland Improved Dwellings Company Ltd...agent for the Gresham Life Assurance Co., the Ocean Accident & Guarantee Corporation Ltd. and Liverpool & London Globe Insurance Co.

c) Shimmin was keen on dating some of his mineral water bottles and although mineral water manufacture at Burnville Road is only listed in directories from 1905 his earliest dated bottle is an aqua Skittle-Codd embossed 1902. *The Mineral Water Trade Journal* March 1903 noted:

Mr. Shimmin of Sunderland is putting up a nice, compact, little factory, everything A1 and when finished it will have an up-to-date appearance; no spoiling of it for the "pennorth" of tar.

Although also running an electro-plating works at Burnville Road from 1905, as seen in the advertisement shown from the *Sunderland Year Book* of that year, he was still making mineral waters in 1907 as *The Mineral Water Trade Journal* December 1907 recorded the prosecution of three youths for breaking into his mineral water manufactory that year.

Shimmin's advertisement in the Sunderland Year Book 1905

d) All was not well in his business ventures however and *The Durham Chronicle* 10 November 1909 reported the appearance of George Shimmin, aged 60, at Durham Assizes before

Justice Walton. He had pleaded guilty to embezzlement and falsifying accounts when acting as secretary of the Starr-Bowkett Building Society and two other societies. The sums amounted to £734 8s 4d but the total amount discovered was nearly £7,000. These frauds had been going on for three or four years and the money had gone to help a **mineral water business** which Shimmin also carried on in Sunderland. He was sentenced "to penal servitude for five years":

Commencing at the age of fourteen in the service of the Consett Iron Company he left them with a good testimonial. In 1888 he went to Sunderland and started the Starr-Bowkett Building Society and other societies and for many years they were carried on successfully. He was an abstainer and no gambling or other vice could be attributed to him. Some years ago…he foolishly commenced another business. He had saved a little money and obtained other money on mortgage and with that erected new premises and plant and carried on the business of a mineral water manufacturer. Unfortunately the business was not as prosperous as he hoped and to redeem part of his loss he started an electro-plating business. This did not prove successful and he gave way to temptation to retrieve his position by taking the society's money hoping he would be able to replace it.

(e) A week after the above court case *The Mineral Water Trade Journal* November 1909 advertised the sale of George Shimmin's mineral water manufactory and his "large stock of bottles…" as shown.

f) The 1910 trade directory lists several occupiers at 17 Burnville Road including a baker, an electrical engineer and a G. Bradford brewer. Interestingly George Bradford of Bradford Brothers of Newcastle upon Tyne (q.v.) left that partnership around 1908 and is a possible candidate for the G. Bradford. No new mineral water business however is evident at this site and what became of the stock of Shimmin's bottles that were offered for sale with his business is unknown. After the high profile local court case involving the embezzlement of the savings of local people it is doubtful that bottles with the name Shimmin on them would

Mineral Water Trade Journal advertisement November 1909

have been very marketable locally and it would therefore seem unlikely that they would have been bought by another North East maker for reuse. Perhaps they were dumped on mass or maybe sold to a firm outside of the North East. Their ultimate fate is not known at this time.

* * *

Robert Stephenson, Gateshead

(1) 10oz Codd

This the fourth firm from Gateshead which used blue glass mineral water bottles. Evidence for this 10oz blue Codd from Robert Stephenson of Gateshead first appeared in the early months of 2013 and consisted of most of the bottom half of a deep blue example. A second example, more complete but still lacking its top, appeared on the market in early 2015. The front is embossed with an oval design enclosing the name **Robt Stephenson** and the town name **Gateshead.** The centre of the design is blank. The maker's name embossed on the lower back is **A. Alexander & Co/ Makers/ Blaydon & London** and the base is embossed **A10**. The appearance of the blue Robert Stephenson standard Codd brings the total of North East firms known to have used blue codds to five the others being Emmerson Brothers of Newcastle upon Tyne, J. Kershaw & Sons of Gateshead, E. J. Stewart of West Hartlepool and Shimmin of Sunderland. The more complete example of the Stephenson Codd is illustrated as found.

Robert Stephenson Gateshead Codd

Notes:
a)   The firm's proprietor is listed in Gateshead as a mineral water manufacturer:
  • 1895-1905 Robert Stephenson, Back James Street
  • 1906 Robert Stephenson, Back James Street and 51 & 53 Bensham Road
b)   All the listings give the proprietor's name as Robert Stephenson apart from in 1905 when the name is Robert H. Stephenson.
c)   Robert Stephenson is listed as living at 105 Redheugh Road 1895-1900 and at 34 James Street (adjacent to the manufactory) 1901-05.

d) The 1901 census lists a Robert Hy Stephenson, born in Sunderland, an unmarried mineral water manufacturer, aged 37 living alone at 34 James Street Gateshead.

e) Back James Street in the period in question only had between three and five unnumbered businesses listed on it. In 1907 no new mineral water maker appears at the Back James Street location of Stephenson.

f) Robert Stephenson used quite a range of coloured Codds all of which are very rare. They include this 10oz blue example, a very rare 10oz green standard Codd with exactly the same embossing seen on the blue example, a rare dumpy amber Codd and an even rarer dumpy emerald green Codd (one incomplete example only is known).

g) He used at least two trade-marks – a bottle (looking something like an apothecary's bottle) and a horse's head beneath a horseshoe both known only on aqua glass mineral water bottles.

* * *

E. J. Stewart, West Hartlepool

(1) 6oz Codd (Trade Mark Registered)
(2) 10oz Codd (Trade Mark Registered)
(3) 10oz Codd (Trade Mark)

A single obscure firm from West Hartlepool on the North East coast of Co. Durham used blue Codds that are considered by many collectors, me included, to be the most desirable blue glass mineral water bottles in the country. The firm was, of course, the celebrated E. J. Stewart of West Hartlepool.

Three types of blue Codds are currently known from the firm and common to all three is the firm's trade mark which looks somewhat like a hamilton with legs and wings but has traditionally been called a dragonfly although it is not a strictly accurate depiction of one. It has also been suggested that it could represent a bluebottle fly which would fit nicely with the colour of the bottles in question. No application to register it as a trade mark was found so we don't have Stewart's own take on the design but I have stayed with the traditional dragonfly description. Above the trade mark is the name of the bottler **E. J. Stewart** and **Trade Mark** with the town name **West Hartlepool** below it.

Types (1) and (2) also have the word **Registered** below the trade mark. Type (3) lacks the word registered. All three types have the maker's details **E. Breffit & Co Ld/ Makers/ Castleford** in three lines at the bottom of the back. Bases of examples of type (1) have the number **9458** embossed and bases of types (2) and (3) the number **9656**.

A single whole example of the 6oz size type (1) was dug in Hartlepool in the early 1970s by a local digger and his sons. This was bought by a bottle dealer Tony Reynolds for the collector and magazine publisher Roy Morgan who was told that the diggers had found no less than nineteen broken examples of both sizes but only the one complete 6oz example. This was first pictured on the cover of Roy Morgan's book *Mainly Coddswallop* in 1974 and it later appeared on the cover of Roger Green's booklet *Old Bottles Year Book 1976-77* and in the first issue of Roy's own magazine *Finders Keepers* in 1980. It remained with Roy Morgan until 1988 when it passed to collector Peter Savage who bought much of Roy's collection (mainly to acquire the blue Hartlepool Codd it was said). It next appeared on the market in 1999 and for a short time was in a North East collection when I got the chance to photograph it before it once more moved to a southern collection.

Incomplete examples of 10oz size Codds have appeared intermittently over the years, albeit rarely, and there are one or two restored examples in circulation but it wasn't until late 2007 early 2008 when a previously unknown ash-tip in Hartlepool was opened up that a whole very sick 10oz example type (3) was found as well as incomplete examples of the 10oz type (2). In fact quite a few fragments came from this tip including a nearly whole 6oz example (type 1) with only part of the lip missing but no more whole examples that I am aware of which leaves the only complete examples documented at this time as the one 6oz type (1) and one 10oz type (3). It would seem logical that a fourth type should exist, namely a 6oz Codd embossed with the words Trade Mark but without the word Registered but all the 6oz fragments dug in 2007 that I have seen were of type (1). All three types are illustrated.

Notes:

a)   Trade directory, family history and census research gives us the following summary of E. J. Stewart's mineral water business in West Hartlepool (see notes (c) and (d) below):

- 1899-1900 E. J. Stewart, mineral water manufacturer, 28 Mosley Street

The proprietor is listed in trade directories as Ernest John Stewart living at 27 Burbank Street West Hartlepool.

b)   Mosley Street in West Hartlepool is shown on the 1896 OS map page 150. The numbering of the street as detailed in trade directories suggests that Stewart's manufactory at number 28 was in a building (arrowed on the map) behind the public house (Black Bull) at the end of the street marked "P.H." on the map. The area is now redeveloped.

E. J. Stewart 6oz Codd
type (1)

E. J. Stewart 10oz Codd
type (3)

E. J. Stewart 10oz Codd
type (2)

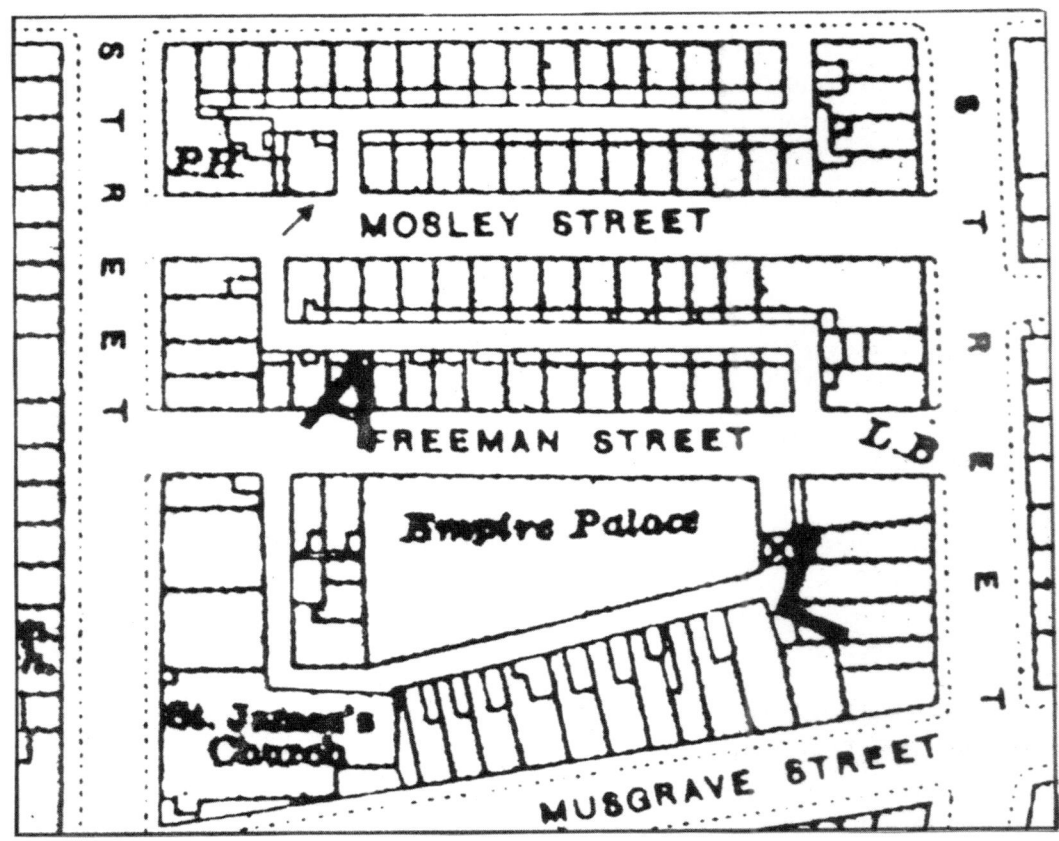

1896 OS map showing Mosley Street

c) E. J. Stewart is only listed as a mineral water manufacturer in the biannual Ward's Directory of 1900-01 (published on 5 July 1900). He is not listed in the previous 1898-1899 edition (which names a hay dealer at 28 Mosley Street) and is likewise not listed in 1902-1903 edition. In the 1904-1905 directory Stewart is listed as a confectioner on Mildred Street and there was an undertaker at the Mosley Street address.

d) E. J. Stewart was born in the September quarter of 1875 in Hartlepool. His mother was Mary Ann Stewart, born in Dover, and his father a master mariner. The 1881 census records Mary Ann Stewart (aged 31) living with her son Ernest John Stewart (aged 5) at 85 Upper Alma Street, Stranton, West Hartlepool. On 19 September 1898 Ernest John Stewart married Susannah Cuthbert in West Hartlepool and their marriage certificate gives his profession as an "Engineer". A daughter, Olive Estella Stewart, was born on 24 August 1899 and her birth certificate gives E. J. Stewart's occupation as "Mineral Water Manufacturer

(Master)". The 1901 census (31 March) records E. J. Stewart as a commission agent for a machinery merchant living with his wife and daughter with his widowed mother, Mary Ann Stewart, a licensed victualler, at the Station Hotel, Edward Street, West Hartlepool (Mick Pickering personal communication).

In summary E. J. Stewart was in business as a mineral water manufacturer for a very short period of time somewhere between September 1898 and March 1901 with a known period from August 1899 to July 1900.

e) Curiously we have no record in the forty years of the hobby of any other types of bottles other than blue Codds from E. J. Stewart. This includes the Hartlepool tip of 2007-08 although with diggers from across the country it would be interesting to know if any were found and have left the North East.

f) Searches of the *Trade Mark Journals* failed to locate an application by E. J. Stewart to register the dragonfly design as a trade mark which may explain the removal of the word Registered from the embossing design.

* * *

P. Thornton (Limited), South Shields

(1) 10oz cylinder (Trade Mark only)
(2) 10oz cylinder (Trade Mark Registered)
(3) 6oz cylinder (P. Thornton Limited)

Peter Thornton's mineral water business in South Shields is well-known to local collectors and is the second firm from the town known to have used blue glass mineral water bottles. Three types are known found in shades ranging from the deepest cobalt to a light cornflower blue and none are common.

Type (1) is a 10oz cylinder with a plain base with a neat 1 inch (25mm) diameter central depression. The body is embossed on one side with the firm's trade mark of a turret with an arm holding a spear all within a circle and the words **Trade Mark**. Above this is **P. Thornton** and below it **South Shields**. The back of the bottle is plain with no maker's details. The trade mark registration details in note (j) below show that this bottle should date to 1872-87.

Type (2) has the same design as type (1) with the addition of the word **Registered** below the trade mark. The trade mark registration details should date this bottle to post-1887.

Type (3) is a 6oz cylinder which is only known as a large piece of the body of an example which came to light in 2010. It has the dimensions of a 6oz cylinder with an unknown lip and is embossed with the firm's trade mark as seen on type (2) along with words **Trade Mark** and **Registered**. The firm's name above the trade mark is **P. Thornton/ Limited** in two lines and below it **South Shields**. At the bottom of the back it has part of the well-known local glass bottle-maker's mark of the **Ayres Quay Bottle Co/ Makers/ Sunderland** and is the only blue glass mineral water bottle known from this major North East glass bottle manufacturer which made so many of the area's iconic mineral water, beer and porter bottles. The use of the word Limited in the firm's title dates this bottle to post-1896 which is the year the limited company was registered. All three types are illustrated.

P. Thornton 10oz cylinder type (1)

P. Thornton 10oz cylinder type (2)

P. Thornton Limited 6oz cylinder type (3)

Notes:

a) Peter Thornton is listed as a mineral water manufacturer, ale porter wine & spirit merchant and licensed victualler in South Shields:

- 1865-1877 3-5 Dixon Street, Laygate Lane
- 1879-1900 Back Thorney Terrace, Laygate Lane
- 1881-1898 Tramcar Hotel, 34 Market Place (victualler)
- 1889-1894 Dining Rooms, 33 Market Place (victualler)
- 1896-1900 The Old Mill, Hardwicke Street

The mineral water works are named as being on Dixon Street in 1873 and from 1879 as on Back Thorney Terrace. The Old Mill on Hardwicke Street is listed under Peter Thornton for ale, porter and stout bottling (see also the limited company registration below).

b) *The Mineral Water Trade Review & Guardian* July 1885 reported that "Mr. Samuel Vincent of South Shields who some short time ago purchased the flourishing business of Mr. Thornton, ale & porter bottler, has added the mineral water department." It is not clear which Thornton this relates to as there were several Thornton family members in the bottling trades in South Shields at this time as well as George Thornton of Jarrow (see note (i) below). Sam Vincent is listed as a mineral water manufacturer, wine, spirit and ale merchant at the Hardwicke Street site 1885-96 (i.e. before Peter Thornton). He moved his business to the Howdon Brewery at Howdon-on-Tyne in 1897.

c) Peter Thornton's firm is listed under the titles:

- 1865-1895 Peter Thornton
- 1896-1900 Peter Thornton Limited

d) *The Mineral Water Trade Review & Guardian* February 1879 published a letter from Peter Thornton giving us the rare chance to read his actual words:

CORKS v. STOPPERS
(To the Editor of the Mineral Water Trade Review and Guardian)

Dear Sir,

In the Trade Memoranda of this month's issue of your paper I observe a paragraph headed "Corks v. Stoppers" which surprises me not a little as I am quite ignorant of any such meeting, as is there referred to, having been held. Nor am I at all aware that the workmen of Shields are at all dissatisfied with the stoppers. I know that my men very much prefer them to corks, and nearly all, if indeed not all, the aërated water makers in North and South Shields have the stoppered bottles; Codd's being most used. There is, however, a feeling against the *prices* of Codd's bottles, myself and other makers being of the opinion that they, as also charge for the license, ought to, and we trust will, be considerably reduced.

Yours truly,

P. Thornton,

South Shields Mineral Water Works, Back Thorney Terrace

d) *The Mineral Water Trade Review and Guardian* August 1879 has a short appraisal of Peter Thornton's mineral water business:

Mr. P. Thornton's Mineral Water Manufactory, South Shields

It was originated some sixteen years ago in a very small and unpretentious manner by the present proprietor's father...The building which is of brick occupies a suitable space of ground at the back of Thorney Terrace which is fitted up with the usual plant for working Codd's patent. Mr Thornton, to his credit be it said, was the first in the town to charge all bottles to the customer as they are delivered.

The census returns detailed below show that Peter Thornton's father was a Richard Thornton who is listed in directories as a grocer, ale and beer retailer at Corstophine Town, South Shields 1856-61.

e) *A Descriptive Account of Newcastle: Illustrated* (c.1894) has a promotional article on Peter Thornton's firm from which the following is an extract:

Mr Peter Thornton
Mineral Water Manufacturer
South Shields Mineral Water Works
Behind Thorney Terrace
Laygate Lane

The business carried on by Mr. Peter Thornton as a mineral water manufacturer was established upwards of thirty years ago...is carried on at the rear of Thorney Terrace in Laygate Lane. The works comprise a two-storied block, range of stabling, cart sheds and a large yard. On the top floor is the laboratory and stores for sugar, essences, carbonate of soda, potass etc. The filtering tanks are two in number of 100 and 150 gallons capacity. Other tanks contain strong solutions of bicarbonate of soda and potass. Then we have the syrup and flavouring tanks connected with the numerous fillers in the room below. In this department we find the Stockport gas engine, a carboniser of large capacity, aerating and filling machinery by Barnett & Foster for bottles, splits and syphons and a McEwan's multiple filler which fills four bottles at the same time and is equal to turn out 100 to 120 dozen bottles per hour. Soda, potass, lemonade, lime juice champagne, ginger beer, ginger ale etc. are of the highest quality. Mr. Thornton also makes a fine quality of fermented ginger beer…and also bottles Bass's ale and Guinness's stout of which large stocks are maintained. Seven horses are employed in delivering the bottles etc. Mr. Thornton has for many years been a member of South Shields Council for Laygate Ward and is also a Guardian of the poor.

f) *The Mineral Water Trade Recorder* May 1896 reported the incorporation of Peter Thornton Limited:

PETER THORNTON, LIMITED

This company was registered on April 14th, with a capital of £3,000 in £10 shares, to acquire and carry on the business of a manufacturer of aerated and mineral waters now carried on by P. Thornton, at Back Thorney Terrace, South Shields, and also the business of a bottler of ale, porter, and stout, carried on at The Old Mill, Hardwick Street, South Shields, and to enter into an agreement with the said Peter Thornton. The subscribers are:- P. Thornton, Thorney Terrace South Shields, manufacturer, one; W.T. Allan, Thorney Terrace, South Shields, manufacturer, one; R.W. Thornton, 4 Malborough Street, South Shields, manufacturer, one; Mrs. R. Thornton, 4 Malborough Terrace, one; Mrs W.T. Allan, Thorney Terrace, South Shields, one; R. Thornton, Gosforth, theatre proprietor, one. The number of directors is not to be less than three nor more than four; qualification £50; remuneration as the Company may decide. Registered by Jordan and Sons, Limited, 120 Chancery Lane, W.C. registered Office, 6 Thorney Terrace, South Shields.

g) After 1899 the business is listed with different titles under two sons of Peter Thornton until 1908:
- 1901-1902 Thornton Brothers
- 1903-1906 Richard Watson Thornton
- 1906-1908 Robert W. Thornton & Co.

From 1909 a P. Tinwell, ale & porter merchant, is listed at Hardwicke Street.

h) The above two notes show that there were several family members involved in the business. Census returns record the following details about Peter Thornton (in bold type) and his family in South Shields (ages in brackets):

- **1851** Richard Thornton (41), grocer, Thornton Street, wife Frances, three daughters and five sons Newton (17), **Peter Thornton** (14), Richard (12), John (8) and George (6).

- **1861** Richard Thornton (51), beer house keeper, Thornton Street, wife Frances, three daughters, and sons **Peter Thornton** (24) railway engine driver, John (18) cartman and George (16) cartman.

- **1871 Peter Thornton** (34), mineral water manufacturer employing 5 men and 4 boys, 5 Dixon Street, wife Isabella, a daughter and a son Richard (5). Another Peter Thornton (18) lemonade bottler, is listed as a brother of Mary Jobling at 6 Dixon Street.

- **1881 Peter Thornton** (44), mineral water manufacturer, 9 Thorney Terrace, wife Isabella, a daughter and two sons Ernest (8) and Robert William (6).

- **1891 Peter Thornton** (54), mineral water manufacturer, 9 Thorney Terrace, wife Isabella, sons Richard W. (34) mineral water manufacturer, Ernest (18), Robert W. (16), nephew Newton G. Thornton (17) engine fitter's apprentice.

- **1901 Peter Thornton** (64), farmer, 9 Thorney Terrace (private house), wife Mary A., son Robert W. (26) mineral water manufacturer.

i) Five other people (including four family members) are listed in directories as involved with Peter Thornton's bottling business:

Richard Thornton

Listed in South Shields:

- 1873-1884 Ale & porter merchant, Laygate Mill, Hardwick Street
- 1881-1888 Innkeeper, Union Alley/ Ferry Street
- 1891-1900 Music Hall proprietor, Union Alley

The theatre on Union Alley is listed as the South Shields Theatre Co. Ltd 1879-1886 and as Thornton's Hall of Varieties 1887-1900. Richard Thornton is thereafter listed as proprietor of the New Empire Palace, King Street (resident in Gosforth). The Hardwicke Street business became part of Peter Thornton Ltd in 1896 with Richard Thornton of Gosforth as a subscriber.

Richard Watson Thornton

Presumed to be a son of Peter Thornton (see the 1891 census above) he is listed as a manager and mineral water manufacturer 1895-1900 and with Mrs R. Thornton of 4 Malborough Crescent as a subscriber in Peter Thornton Ltd in 1896. From 1903-06 the former Peter Thornton business is listed under his name.

Robert W. Thornton & Co.

Presumed to be a son of Peter Thornton (see the 1881-1901 census returns above). From 1906-08 the former Peter Thornton business is listed under his name.

William T. Allan

Listed as the mineral water works manager at 6 Thorney Terrace in 1894 and along with Mrs W. T. Allan he was a subscriber to Peter Thornton Ltd in 1896.

Newton Gray Thornton

Presumed to be Peter Thornton's nephew listed in the 1891 census above. Newton Gray Thornton and Peter Thornton jointly registered the trade mark of a George Thornton, mineral water manufacturer of Jarrow, in 1887. *The Mineral Water Trade Review & Guardian* April 1886 noted the death of George Thornton at the age of 40 which suggests that he was the brother of Peter Thornton (see 1851 and 1861 census returns above). There is no other obvious involvement of George Thornton or Newton Gray Thornton in Peter Thornton's South Shields business.

j) Peter Thornton applied for the turret, arm and spear device as a trade mark in Class 44 (no. 66, 623) on 5 August 1887 claiming its previous use from 1872.

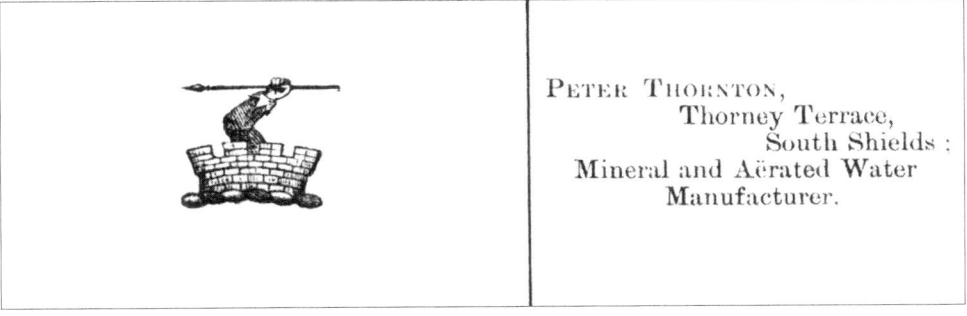

Trade mark registration of Peter Thornton

k) As shown *Kelly's Post Office Trade Directory of Durham* of 1879 contains an advertisement from Peter Thornton showing a trade mark of six men in a boat but registration of this design was not found in the *Trade Mark Journals*. A similar trade mark was used by two other South Shields bottling firms, G. H. Steel and Robert Metcalf, all no doubt in tribute to the town's famous connection with the development of the first lifeboat.

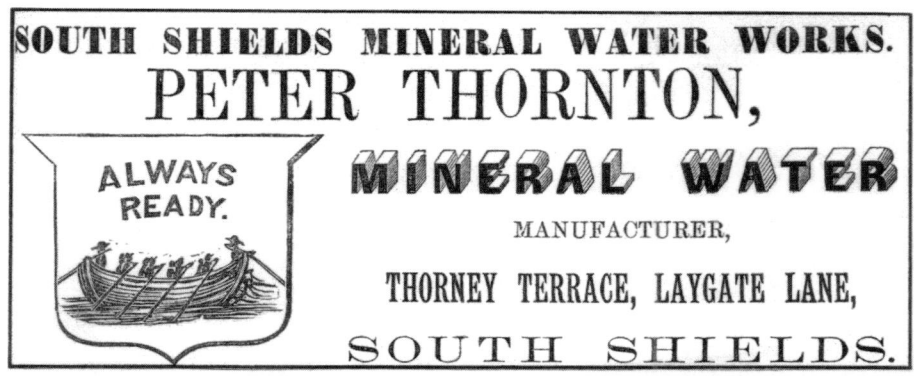

Advertisement from Kelly's Trade Directory of Durham 1879

l) *The Mineral Water Trade Journal* of May 1913 reported the sudden death of Peter Thornton (undated) at his residence Rose Villa in Harton Village. After noting his business as a mineral water manufacturer it also noted that he had "purchased the Tramcar Hotel in the South Shields Market Place; and, after conducting it successfully for a considerable period, disposed of the concern some thirteen or fourteen years ago".

Bibliography

The books and periodicals below have formed the main sources of the information in this book. Specific sources are named in the text.

Barber, Norman 2005 *A Century of British Breweries*

Bennison, Brian 1995 *Brewers & Bottlers of Newcastle upon Tyne* Newcastle upon Tyne

Bennison, Brian 2004 *The Brewers & Breweries of North-Eastern England*

Brand, John 1789 *History & Antiquities of Newcastle*

Chilton, P. & Poppleston, M. c.1978 *The Early Brewing Trade of the Tyne*: unpub. mss.

Douglas, Peter n.d. *Extracts from the Mineral Water Trade Review & Guardian* Vol. 1

Ellis, Richard 1894 *Health Resorts of Northumberland and Durham* London & Newcastle

Ellison, Margaret 1975 *The Tyne Glasshouses and Beilby-Bewick Workshop* A.A. 5 vol. 3

Gosney, Ron n.d. *Glassmaking in Knottingley* www.knottingley.org/history/glassmakers.

Graham, Frank 1969 *Northumberland & Durham: A Social Miscellany* Newcastle

Graham, Frank 1976 *Historic Newcastle* Newcastle

Green, Clifford 1977 *Cleaning Methods, a Dump Diggers Guide* Southampton

Green, Roger 1977 *Old Bottles Year Book 1976-77* Albrighton

Gubbins, Bridget 2011 *The Curious Yards & Alleyways of Morpeth* Morpeth

Lockhart, Shriever, Serr and Lindsey n.d. Society for Historical Archaeology www.sha.org

Morgan, Roy 1974 *Mainly Coddswallop* Wellingborough

Potten, Mark 2006 *Encyclopaedia of Hiram Codd's Globe-Stoppered Bottles* (CD)

Richardson, William 1923 *History of the Parish of Wallsend* Newcastle upon Tyne

Richmond, L. and Turton, A. 1990 *The Brewing Industry* Manchester

Robertson, David 2012 *The North East Bottle Collectors Guide to Newcastle upon Tyne, Gateshead & Surrounding Areas* Broompark

Ross, Catherine 1982 *Development of the Glass Industry on the Rivers Tyne and Wear 1700-1900* (unpublished PhD thesis) 1982

Rush, James 1973 *The Ingenious Beilbys*. Barrie & Jenkins London

Rush, James 1987 *A Beilby Odyssey*. Nelson & Saunders

Simmons, Douglas 1983 *Schweppes the First 200 years* London

Talbot, Olive 1974 *The Evolution of Glass Bottles for Carbonated Drinks*. Post-Medieval Archaeology vol. 8

Tattersfield, Nigel 1999 *Bookplates by Beilby & Bewick* London

Whellan, Francis 1894 *History, Topography and Directory of Durham* (Second edition)

Trade periodicals and sources without authors

Aerator and Bottler

A Descriptive Account of Newcastle, Illustrated (c.1894) Brighton

Dictionary of Business Biography volume 2 1984

Glass Making on Wearside 1979 Tyne & Wear County Council Museums

Grace's Guide to British Industrial History 2007

An Illustrated Guide to Sunderland and District Edinburgh & London 1898

The London Gazette

Mineral Water Trade Journal (British & Colonial Mineral Water Trade Journal)

Mineral Water Trade Recorder (Mineral Water Trade Recorder & Bottlers' Advocate)

Mineral Water Trade Review & Guardian

Northumberland at the Opening of the 20th Century 1905 Brighton

Northumberland & Durham Bottle Collectors Club newsletters 1977 to date

Rivers of the North 1894 London

Sunderland Year Books 1905, 1910 Sunderland

Trade Directories of Northumberland and Co. Durham from 1778 to date

Trade Mark Journals

Tyneside Industries 1889 London

(This volume's full title is *The Tyneside: Newcastle District: An Epitome of Results and Manual of Commerce* but it is commonly known as *Tyneside Industries*)

Specialist UK Bottle Magazines

Antique Bottle Collecting

Antique Bottle Collector

Bottles and Bygones

British Bottle Review

Finders Keepers

The earliest national bottle magazines in the United Kingdom are *Antique Bottle Collecting* established in 1975 and running until the early 1980s followed by *British Bottle Review* in 1979. At the time of writing only British Bottle Review and Antique Bottle Collector (established in 2000) are still being published.

Appendix

The following is an alphabetical checklist of the North East firms that appear in this book along with a summary of the types of blue glass mineral water bottles that they used. All the bottles have blob-tops unless stated otherwise. Abbreviations of embossing variations, as detailed under each individual firm in chapter 5, are given when appropriate. Details in square brackets are bottle-maker's details where these appear on the bottles.

John Arkle, Morpeth, Northumberland

Type (1) 6oz Hamilton
Type (2) 10oz Hamilton

John J. Bell, Newcastle upon Tyne

Type (1) 10oz Hamilton

Bewick Bros, Blaydon, Co. Durham

Type (1) 6oz Hamilton
Type (2) 10oz Hamilton

F. Bradford, Newcastle upon Tyne

Type (1) 6oz Hamilton
Type (2) 10oz Hamilton
Type (3) 6oz flat-bottomed Hamilton
Type (4) 10oz flat-bottomed Hamilton

Bradford Bros, Newcastle upon Tyne

Type (1) 6oz flat-bottomed Hamilton
Type (2) 10oz flat-bottomed Hamilton
Type (3) 10oz flat-bottomed crown-cap Hamilton

Crystal Aerated Water Co., Newcastle upon Tyne

Type (1) 10oz Hamilton

J. Deuchar, Newcastle upon Tyne

Type (1) 10oz Hamilton

Dowson Brothers, Gateshead, Co. Durham

Type (1) 10oz round-bottomed cylinder

G. Eland, Newcastle upon Tyne

Type (1) 10oz Hamilton (GE's/PW/CS – N/ Established 1837)

Type (2) 10oz Hamilton (GE's/PW/CS/WR/N – Established 1837/ TM) (chisel-lip)

Type (3) 10oz Hamilton (GE's/PW/CS/WR/N – Established 1837/ TM)

Type (4) 6oz Hamilton (GE's/MW/CS/WR/N – Established 1837/ TM)

Type (5) 6oz Hamilton (GE/CS/N – Established 1837/TM)

Type (6) 6oz Hamilton (GE/CS/N – Established 1837/TM) (chisel-lip)

Type (7) 10oz Hamilton (GE's/SW/CS/WR/N – Established 1837/ TM) (chisel-lip)

Type (8) 10 oz Hamilton (GE's/PW/N – TM)

Type (9) 10oz Hamilton (GE's/PW/CS/WR/N – TM)

Emmerson Bros, Newcastle upon Tyne

Type (1) 6oz cylinder

Type (2) 6oz Patent Safe Groove Codd [Dan Rylands]

R.Emmerson Jnr, Newcastle upon Tyne

Small Trade Mark

    Type (1) 6oz cylinder (A10 on the base)

    Type (2) 6oz cylinder (plain base)

    Type (3) 6oz cylinder (chisel-lip, plain base)

    Type (4) 10oz cylinder (plain base)

    Type (5) 10oz cylinder (chisel-lip, plain base)

Large Trade Mark

    Type (6) 6oz cylinder (plain base)

    Type (7) 10oz cylinder (A10 on the base)

    Type (8) 10oz round-bottomed cylinder

Open Trade Mark

    Type (9) 10oz Hamilton

Fleet, Birtley, Co. Durham
Type (1) 10oz cylinder

Walter Forbes, Edinburgh & Newcastle
Type (1) 10oz cylinder

Gilpin & Co., Newcastle upon Tyne
Type (1) 10oz Hamilton (Gilpin & Co/ 101 Pilgrim St/ Newcastle on Tyne – plain)
Type (2) 10oz Hamilton (Gilpin & Co/ Estab. 1790/ 137 Pilgrim St – Newcastle on Tyne)
Type (3) 10oz Hamilton (Gilpin/ Newcastle – Potass / Water) (chisel-lip)
Type (4) 10oz Hamilton (Gilpin/ Newcastle – Potass / Water)
Type (5) 10oz Hamilton (Gilpin & Co/ 137 Pilgrim St/ Newcastle on Tyne – Estab. 1790)
Type (6) 10oz flat-bottomed Hamilton (Gilpin & Co – Established 1790)
Type (7) 10oz Hamilton (etched)

Glendenning, Newcastle upon Tyne
Type (1) 6oz round-bottomed cylinder
Type (2) 10oz Hamilton

J. G. Graham, Newcastle upon Tyne
Type (1) 10oz Hamilton

Jas. Grieves (& Sons), South Shields, Co. Durham
Type (1) 10oz cylinder (James Grieves)
Type (2) 6oz cylinder (James Grieves & Sons) [4]

Hornsby Bros, Gateshead, Co. Durham
Type (1) 10oz flat-bottomed Hamilton

J. Kershaw & Sons, Gateshead, Co. Durham
Type (1) 10oz ginger beer shape
Type (2) Four-way patent internal stopper [Dan Rylands]

Jas McKie & Son(s), Newcastle upon Tyne
Jas McKie & Son

Type (1) 6oz cylinder

Type (2) 10oz round-bottomed cylinder

Type (3) 10oz Hamilton

Type (4) 10oz Hamilton (etched)

Jas McKie & Sons

Type (5) 6oz cylinder

Type (6) 10oz round-bottomed cylinder

Newcastle & District Aerated Water Co., Newcastle upon Tyne

Type (1) 6oz flat-bottomed Hamilton

Type (2) 10oz flat-bottomed Hamilton

W. B. Reid & Co. Ltd, Newcastle upon Tyne

Type (1) 6oz cylinder [A. A. & Co.]

Type (2) 10oz cylinder [A. A. & Co.]

Type (3) 10oz cylinder [R. B. B.]

William Robson, Sunderland, Co. Durham

Type (1) 10oz champagne shape screw-stopper [B & Co Ltd K]

W. Roome, Darlington, Co. Durham

Type (1) 10oz Hamilton

Ross & Co., Newcastle upon Tyne

Type (1) 6oz flat-bottomed Hamilton

Type (2) 10oz flat-bottomed Hamilton

William Row, Newcastle upon Tyne

Type (1) 6oz round-bottomed cylinder (with word Registered)

Type (2) 10oz round-bottomed cylinder (without the word Registered)

G. T. Scott & Co., Wallsend, Northumberland

Type (1) 6oz cylinder

Type (2) 10oz cylinder

Shimmin, Sunderland, Co. Durham

Type (1) 6oz Skittle Codd [Dobson & Nall Ltd]

Robert Stephenson, Gateshead, Co. Durham

Type (1) 10oz Codd [A. Alexander & Co.]

E. J. Stewart, West Hartlepool, Co Durham

Type (1) 6oz Codd (with the word Registered) [E. Breffit & Co. Ld]

Type (2) 10oz Codd (with the word Registered) [E. Breffit & Co. Ld]

Type (3) 10oz Codd (without the word Registered) [E. Breffit & Co. Ld]

P. Thornton (Limited), South Shields

Type (1) 10oz cylinder (without the word Registered)

Type (2) 10oz cylinder (with the word Registered)

Type (3) 6oz cylinder (P. Thornton Limited) [Ayres Quay Bottle Company]